LEADING EDGE
Business
Planning For
Entrepreneurs

JAMES ARKEBAUER
JACK MILLER

DEARBORN™
A **Kaplan Professional** Company

Editorial Director: Jean Iversen
Managing Editor: Jack Kiburz
Project Editor: Trey Thoelcke
Interior Design: Lucy Jenkins
Cover Design: The Publishing Services Group
Typesetting: Elizabeth Pitts

©1999 by James Arkebauer and Jack Miller

Published by Dearborn,
A Kaplan Professional Company

Printed in the United States of America

99 00 01 10 9 8 7 6 5 4 3 2 1

Library of Congress Cataloging-in-Publication Data

Arkebauer, James B., 1939–
    Leading edge business planning for entrepreneurs / James
Arkebauer, Jack Miller.
       p.   cm.
    Includes index.
    ISBN 1-57410-117-X
    1. New business enterprises—Management.   2. Stocks—Entrepreneurship.
3. Success in business..   I. Miller, Jack, 1949–   II. Title.
III. Title: Business planning for entrepreneurs.
HD62.5.A738   1999
658.4′012—dc21   98-52091
                                       CIP

Dedication

To Sara and Brutus and those who love them.

Contents

Preface

About This Book

Entrepreneurs are starting new types of companies that differ radically from the enterprises of just a few years ago. These new companies are typically smaller, and often self- or internally funded. They rely on information, innovation, or both. They are more flexible, change regularly, and have fewer employees than older traditional companies.

The rise of smaller companies—coupled with entrepreneurial turnover and the growing reliance on telecommunications, global marketing, the Internet, and virtual operations—has led to changes in the nature of the underlying business plans that form their foundations. This book reflects many of these changes. We wrote it for the entrepreneurs of Leading Edge, innovative companies who may know a lot about their industry or product, but less about the many new options and decisions on structuring their companies and determining their operational courses.

Leading Edge Business Planning for Entrepreneurs has sixteen chapters. Each chapter discusses a major area or need of business plan writing. Most entrepreneurs need to study each chapter or, at minimum, review the highlights. All chapters are applicable regardless of whether you are contemplating starting an internally funded business, or seeking guidance to assist you in improving the organization, increasing its performance, or finding additional financing. The Epilogue offers a wrap-up and the Appendix contains sample plans.

Chapter 1, The New Business World, discusses the new styles of entrepreneurial companies, the environment in which they are created, and the circumstances and nature of starting a business in the United States as we enter a new century.

Chapter 2, Why You Need a Business Plan, discusses the need for business planning, the purpose and contents of a plan, and how a Leading Edge business plan can help you picture a complete company and get it funded.

Chapter 3, The Prefeasibility Test, checks your business idea to help turn your vision into a business concept. You will get a more complete picture of your business, and see if your idea has the potential to make a profit. It points to areas where you need more definition, but most importantly, it starts the process of business planning on paper.

Chapter 4, Research, teaches the methods, sources, locations, and techniques to find the information you need to make assumptions, projections, and plans for your industry and markets.

Chapter 5, The Feasibility Study, shows you how to run a study that determines who your market is; how much of a demand it generates; forecast sales based on this demand; and the costs, revenues, and returns on investment that you can expect.

Chapter 6, Testing Reality, shows three management tools that help you find your company's strengths and weaknesses in its industry, and figure out the most important factors your business must accomplish if it is to be successful.

Chapter 7, Writing a Leading Edge Business Plan, presents nine guiding principles to incorporate into your business plan writing. It discusses choices and sources of financing, plus how Leading Edge entrepreneurs use combinations of these. It presents the stages of entrepreneurial development to help you determine which stage applies to your business.

Chapter 8, Setting Up Your Leading Edge Plan, shows you how to format your business plan, presents a main heading outline, and shows how to write a cover sheet and an executive summary. Today's plans must be succinct, clear, understandable, and to the point, while covering a lot of ground.

Chapter 9, The Business Description, defines the business, its history (which every startup has), its owners, products or services, and what makes the company unique.

In Chapter 10, Products or Services, you learn how to present the company's products or services, how to add value, how to show and protect their unique features and innovations, and what makes them appealing to your customers or special or unique in your markets.

Chapter 11 covers the market. Every company has a market, and you must unveil the secrets of preparing customer, industry, and competitive market profiles.

After you've told your business plan reader all about your market, you then have to concentrate on an area that most business plans miss. Chapter 12, The Marketing Strategy, details how to develop a marketing strategy to optimize your market share. It shows you how to present your strategy in a Leading Edge way.

The management team is the most important part of every business and Chapter 13, The Leading Edge Management Team, tells you what you need in your team and how to demonstrate that you understand this major business need. It helps you include some management players you may not have thought about before.

Business plan writing is about strutting your stuff, and the most important "stuff" you strut is how you present your financials. Chapter 14, The Financials, guides you through the proper and improper ways to present your financials persuasively.

Chapter 15, The Operations Plan, helps you set milestones and figure out business tasks—the nuts and bolts of operations, ways to describe your facilities, research and development, policies and processes, and determine some of the risk factors that come with starting a business.

The final chapter, Chapter 16, Support Documents, addresses how to treat the appendix in your plan, including what support documents you should include in your plan. Additionally, you'll find some final planning points, and some hints on what investors look for when they are reviewing your plan.

The Epilogue gives you a round-up on the need for and benefits of business planning.

Appendix: Summary Business Plans, presents four different styles for different types of enterprises. You will find the different approaches useful in showing there is no single completely correct way to develop a business plan. At the same time, the primary business plan subjects are covered in each plan.

Entrepreneurs have been a major force in our business environment for centuries. During the last decade, this business environment has changed considerably and we are all faced with learning and adopting new methods to carry on our chosen area of commerce. You will find this book packed with helpful ideas and a lot of food for thought to assist you in becoming a Leading Edge entrepreneur. Please accept our best wishes as you start your Leading Edge journey.

Acknowledgments

Today's entrepreneur harks back to the early days of our country. Pioneering men and women started private enterprises, many from their homes or as solo operators. History repeats itself. Although many of today's entrepreneurs still contend with the kids and pets interrupting their livelihood, they also have space age electronic technology and thousands of new, world-wide market choices and options.

As business consultants and authors, we are exposed to hundreds of Leading Edge entrepreneurs in our daily lives. We thank them for helping us write this book. We learn from them and the people they write plans for give us valuable feedback that we in turn are passing on to you, the reader. We appreciate your feedback.

Jim Arkebauer thanks his clients for putting up with his time-consuming obsession to write this book. He also expresses great appreciation to Maita Lester, an entrepreneur and life partner.

Jack Miller wishes to thank his family, friends, and clients—who probably put up with more than they expected so that he could write this book.

Both of us would like to thank you, the entrepreneurs who enrich our lives daily.

If you wish to contact us to inquire or comment, we suggest you do so through our World Wide Web site: www.venturea.com, or e-mail Jack Miller at infopr@worldnet.att.net.

1

The New Business World

A New Kind of Startup

It took more money, time, and effort to start companies 20 years ago, even 10 years ago, than it does today. During the 1970s and for much of the 1980s, new companies were planned around the concept of permanent employees working at company owned facilities.

New firms were bigger and designed to exist much longer. The family enterprise would grow to include more locations and more employees. It would operate for decades with each generation enjoying greater market share, employing more people, and diversifying locations and product offerings.

The entrance barrier to starting this type of firm was high. Buildings, people, and machinery cost a lot of money. The effort to put a company together using these components took time. The high costs associated with employees, equipment, and buildings required all new companies to be funded with considerable capital, typically from investment banks, venture capital firms, or stock subscriptions.

The new company wrote a business plan to gain outside investor interest. These financing business plans were built on a model showing how the company justified its revenue streams.

Prior to the mid-1990s, venture capitalists seldom looked at plans asking for less than a million dollars in new company financing. The funding process often took six months, a year, or even longer.

The Impact of Technology

Microchips, computers, telecommunications, the Internet, and a host of technology have changed the rules. New companies can be formed to compete in most industries with just one, or a few, employees. To be profitable, a company does not need a physical office location. It does not have to make a product or provide a service directly. It can merely link to other companies that manufacture, sell, store, ship, distribute, publish, or in some other way, offer better methods to put desired products or services into its customers' hands.

The advent of virtual offices, production, promotion, distribution, and sales—where outside firms undertake business processes previously done internally—have annihilated literally every business concept dating back more than five years. The previous model of three to five years to profitability, based on people and buildings, is obsolete.

Information technology makes it possible for today's entrepreneurs to open and operate much more nimble companies. An entrepreneur can start a company with a good idea and some industry or product knowledge. Essential personnel, management advice, facilities, products, and services come from software and experts or information sources *outside* the company. This saves money, time, and complexity—all of which helps lower the entrance barriers to starting a company and obtaining rapid profitability.

Information Fuels Innovative Companies

At the turn of the twenty-first century, the typical product cycle runs from 12 to 18 months. A new company must return a quick profit—before the entrepreneur's knowledge, connections, or other information-based key success factors become obsolete.

This short funding cycle prevents investors from funding research. The twenty-first century growth company either self-funds, or at the very least, demonstrates the business concept and commences operations before its owner can look for outside funding.

The Leading Edge entrepreneur manages information to reach her business goals. Low cost, accurate information—applied throughout the business planning process—is essential to business success, more so today than ever before. This book is based on the concept of finding, applying, and using timely, accurate information to benefit your company at every step in the planning process.

Do not be alarmed. The fast growth of information also has improved the ease and cost of being able to acquire and use information—especially for people who do not feel technically capable. Computer prices have fallen well below $1,000 for better desktop machines than those used by Fortune 1000 companies ten years ago. Libraries in the United States routinely offer easy, free, or very low-cost searches of powerful information databases.

During the 1960s and 1970s large firms maintained private libraries and contracted with researchers to access the most up-to-date information for the company's needs. Today an amazing amount of this type and quality of information is available through free or low costs sources—by telephone, from libraries, and increasingly from the Internet.

The Rise of the Leading Edge Company

All these changes, from the questioning of the '60s, corporate downsizing in the '70s and '80s, and the technology explosion of the '90s, has led to a new type of startup: the Leading Edge company. Leading Edge companies start smaller, operate leaner, and take advantage of technology. They operate, at least for a time, from a small office or space, usually found in a home.

Leading Edge companies have few employees. They use computers, telecommunications technology, the Internet, virtual processes, personal counselors, outside advisers and consultants, temporary services, and other resources to leverage and operate an entire company with few employees—usually less than five.

A Leading Edge company may run full time or part time. Profit is not the only goal. Personal satisfaction or "quality time" in the home is the hallmark of success for many of these newer, smaller companies. They may operate from office or home, on a computer's hard drive, or in a "virtual" mode, with no offices or employees. A growing number run all their marketing and sales electronically.

Careful planning and application of knowledge and technology permit Leading Edge companies to successfully compete on a local, regional, national, or international basis. Leading Edge companies create, design, locate, assemble, sell, store, and distribute literally every product and service imaginable. They operate at all levels and across most presently defined industry boundaries.

Where You Fit into the Picture

No matter what you think, these changes affect your new company, lowering the barriers to startup and making it more complex at the same time. The Internet will become the largest marketplace in the world within five years, even though it is still so new that few standard operating practices exist.

A successful online startup can be bought out within one to two years, before it generates a dollar in revenues or turns a profit. Other companies will be destroyed by changes in technology, markets, or the nature of business.

What all this means is that entrepreneurs today have to consider the many types, methods, concepts, technology options, and operating assumptions to operate a business that were unavailable at the beginning of the decade. The level of thought and complexity offer more opportunities for success and for failure. The good new is that there is more help, more easily available, than ever before. One hallmark of the Leading Edge entrepreneur is to take advantage of that help.

2

Why You Need a Business Plan

Business Planning Is Essential

Most successful companies operate according to some form of plan. A good plan works from a model, which is using good information and mathematical assumptions. The information and assumptions used depend on the goals and desires of the entrepreneurial team starting the company.

Which brings us back to the need for planning, a concept that many people attempt to shortcut, if not ignore. To gain a better understanding of why planning a business is important, look at the example below. Although it is very simple, it presents an important concept: the need to picture a company before starting it. Try using this example with your own numbers.

The $36,000 Question
• • • • •

Imagine you wish to start your own company. To survive financially, you must take in at least twice the minimum wage for every moment the company operates. To save money, you run the company from home. You have no employees. $10,000 will start things off nicely, so you use your personal savings to finance the company. How big is your first year risk to go into business?

The main purpose of most business plans is to justify the new company's revenues, so if you take . . .

$12.50/hour × 40 hours per week × 52 weeks/year	=	$26,000
+ Startup expenses	+	10,000
This leads to a minimum investment risk of		$36,000

That's right! At the turn of the coming century, your decision to start a business, while cutting expenses to the bone and using up your savings, involves a $36,000 decision, unless you want to open a lemonade stand. It is your money, and usually your family and personal sanity, on the line. For this level of risk, planning in advance pays.

Knowing that your personal decision is much larger than $36,000, ask yourself, "Do I want to be in business for myself next year?" If the answer is, "Yes, my goal is to start my own business within a year," or, "Yes, I want to stay in business, I want to grow," then you have no choice but to write a business plan. The good news is that this is a lot easier than you think. Planning simply means *getting organized*, something this book will help you do so step-by-step.

Does this sound like you? Everybody wants to see your business plan. You do not have a plan and you dread the idea of putting one together. You are not sure what to write, let alone know how to write a business plan.

If you are thinking about starting a company, you have probably had your attorney, accountant, and some potential investors or your in-laws ask about your business plan. If you are already running your own company, the person requesting your plan may be a venture capitalist, a banker, or a prospective top-notch employee.

Business Plans Fill Two Purposes

It does not make any difference if you are a mom-and-pop start-up, or an existing high-tech company looking to expand. There are two primary purposes to a business plan:

1. Obtain funding. There's no business without the bucks.
2. Provide a foundation for early development; to keep the entrepreneurial business itself and all its decision makers headed toward its predetermined objectives.

For business planning purposes, the challenge is to explain in an engaging way, with interesting information, how the company will be run for the next one to five years. The entrepreneur must put all the "how" and "needs" together into one neat package. The human and physical resources must correlate with the marketing, operational, and financial strategies of the company. Even if an entrepreneur has magical powers of persuasion, this is not the time to try to fake it.

Your business plan is a vital sales tool for approaching and capturing financial sources, be they investors or lenders. The people funding a business want to know that the entrepreneurial team has thought through the plan carefully. They want to be convinced that your team has the skills and expertise needed to actively manage the company and that the team is prepared to seize opportunities and solve the problems that arise.

The Leading Edge Difference

It cannot be stressed too strongly that a good business plan is the cornerstone of successful financing. If you want investors' money, you've got to give them good reasons to invest in you and your business. The business plan is where you lay out the reasons. It doesn't have to be lengthy or complicated, but it must be informative, relevant, and complete. It needs to maintain logic and order, and show how the company is effectively positioned as a good investment. So your business plan must be well prepared, professional in tone, and persuasive in conveying the company's potential—even if you intend to fund the company yourself.

Operate Your Business on Paper

Business plans boil down to operating the company on paper. The aim is to validate an idea and challenge every aspect of the business. A business plan is a written presentation that carefully explains the business, its management team, its products or services, and its goals—together with strategies for reaching the goals.

Writing the plan may be a painstaking process, but keep in mind that your business plan is the picture and the sales tool for your company. It requires careful consideration of all the multiple facets of a start-up or business expansion. It cannot be written as an afterthought, and it should not be taken lightly.

Check with any professional investor anywhere in the country and you will hear horror stories about ill conceived, poorly written, or sloppily put together business plans. As great as the company's potential may be, it is essentially doomed to rejection before it can even get a foot in the door if it has a poorly conceived business plan.

Focus

There are a number of differences between a Leading Edge business plan and its ordinary counterparts. We'll be pointing them out as we go along. But the first major point is that your business plan will be directed to a specific type of funding source and written to address and satisfy that source's particular concerns.

For example, you would orient and write the plan differently for presentation to a banker than you would for a venture capitalist, an underwriter, or a private investor. The banker wants more information about how good the security and collateral is, whereas the venture capitalist wants to know what risks are involved. These concerns must be individually addressed. There are no hard and fast rules for preparing a business plan. The key word is *ingenuity*. Strive for inventiveness, strive to be interesting and captivating. Focus on a specific reader by customizing your approach in the plan.

Another Leading Edge Difference

Another Leading Edge business planning point is to recognize that constant change is inevitable. These changes, coming both from success and setbacks, require that the business plan be almost constantly updated and that the document is flexible. Quarterly reviews may not be enough. Updates may have to be done every six weeks.

Leading Edge entrepreneurs are always making progress or subtle changes of direction in their companies. It may come with a new contract, a new product approval, a successful beta test, or a new member of the management team. Regardless, one will fast discover that a business plan often goes stale—even as the first copies go out the door.

Make simple update sheets as supplements to a plan. Further, revise the plan as often as necessary. It is your blueprint to success. That is why it is so important that the key members of the entrepreneurial team be intimately involved in business plan writing and revisions. This ongoing revision process brings home the strategic value that both the management team and the plan play in assuring that everyone is singing from the same songbook.

Your Plan Takes Effort

Each company is different and your plan must be tailor-made to fit your particular situation. The ideal business plan just does not exist, and generic software-based business plan templates fail to do the trick. Expect to spend a minimum of two to three months and 200 to 300 hours writing your plan. It's not unheard of that an entrepreneur spends up to a year putting together a detailed plan. Additionally, you'll have to spend some time in preparing and rehearsing your oral pitch to investors. Remember that your words and story not only have to paint a pretty picture, they must be persuasive and practical as well.

Don't approach writing the business plan as a necessary evil. Rather, look at it as a helpful tool that can be used to exploit the advantages of your product or service.

What You Will Learn

Make it your rule that you *must* have an up-to-date business plan. Just like you have to get a business license or renew an incorporation or patent, you need to periodically evaluate all aspects of your business. Financiers want to see a written plan, and your self-imposed rule means you'll be ready for every opportunity. It will pay off!

The business plan provides a necessary look at the details of the business. Simply, it includes: an examination of the products or services (advantages), the market (customers), the industry (competitors), marketing (distribution and pricing), production (operations), management (people), and financing (equity/debt structure). It notes each activity's, time and costs. What your plan tells its readers, including yourself, is: "Here is what we propose to do, this is how we are going to achieve it with what resources."

You Are the Responsible Party

This book provides you with all the basics you will need to write a Leading Edge business plan. However, you are the one who will have to assume the responsibility to do the actual plan. Others can assist you with research, brainstorming ideas, and writing, but you will have to get into a lot of the nitty-gritty details yourself. After all, it is your idea, your company, and your vision.

You do not have to go through this whole process alone, nor should you. Venture capitalists frequently work with entrepreneurs, over extended periods of time, consulting with them on the writing of their business plans. These plans often go through numerous revisions. It is not unusual to revise a business plan six to ten times before showing it to the first potential investor. As it is a living document, expect to revise parts of the plan many times in the future.

Most accounting firms will help you with your financials and some local colleges will assist you in identifying a student who has business plan writing skills and would be pleased to have extra income. Some state governments have set up Small Business Development Centers (SBDCs) to assist you in putting together business plans.

However, if you seek outside assistance, you must furnish complete information for the plan. You know what is and is not important about your business. You live it every day, right there on the firing line. You have the emotion inside you that only you can portray to the reader.

The outside consultant should be a specialist in ways to create an interesting and easy-to-read plan. However, more important is her ability to assist you in the numerous revisions you will have to make. Good business plan writing is heavy-duty editing and rewriting.

Before you send out finished copies of your plan, have some other people whose opinion you respect read and review your plan. Be sure to check for misspellings, typos, and sloppy word smithing. The future of your business depends upon the quality of your Leading Edge plan.

3 The Prefeasibility Test

Through the course of life each of us may dream up a number of business ideas. We know the idea is serious when it becomes a vision that consumes us.

We then ask questions like: How do I know if my business idea makes sense? Does my dream have the potential to make money? Because the business planning process is so involved, we have created a short, easy Prefeasibility Test to help you separate a business idea from fantasy.

The test is based on what you know right now. If you take the time to answer the questions below, you can learn two things about your business concept:

1. Do you have, or are you willing to get, a deep understanding of your business concept?
2. Does your concept, as you see it, have a chance to earn a profit?

Do not worry about the completeness of your answers. The idea behind this test is for you to spend a few minutes thinking about and picturing your concept as an actual business.

Although taking this test may seem like a lot of work, the amount of information you put into your answers have a direct bearing on how much you can accept the results. If you start with a minimal idea, your answers will probably be way off the mark, in which case you gain a better understanding of what you need to do to start your company. You will get the most value from the Prefeasibility Test if you are very honest with your answers and your assessment of those answers.

An incomplete or "I don't know" means your idea needs work. Some of you may not initially understand the concept of costs or expenses related to a particular activity or item. Do not be alarmed. The chapters on research, feasibility, and testing in this section—plus the marketing, finance, and other topics in Chapters 4 through 6—add a lot of details.

The Prefeasibility Test

Discover the extent of your business vision.

1. Write a brief description of your company. Include the items below, plus any other information you already have in mind.

    a. Where is it located?

    b. What do you sell?

    c. Who are your customers?

    d. How do you make sales?

    e. Who else works there?

    f. What activities take place on a typical day?

2. What products or services will your company sell? How much will you charge for each?

    Brief Description of Product or Service   Price

    a. _____ $_____

    b. _____ $_____

    c. _____ $_____

3. How many times will your company sell each product or service in a month? (If you sell something only a few times per year, then fill in your yearly sales below and do not by multiply by the number of months in question 4 below). If you are unsure how many sales you will make, take your best guess.

    | | Number of Times |
Brief Description of Product or Service	Sold per Month
a. _____	_____
b. _____	_____
c. _____	_____

4. How much income will your company make? Assume that there will be no sales until the second month in the first year.

   a. In its first year?
      Multiply question 2 × 3a × 11 (months/year) = \$_____

   b. In its second year?
      Multiply question 2 × 3b × 12 (months/year) = \$_____

5. Where will your company be located? Check all locations your business will use, including virtual facilities or facilities rented from other companies.

   a. In its first year.
      ❑ Home   ❑ Office   ❑ Factory   ❑ Warehouse
      ❑ Shipping   ❑ Computing   ❑ Other _____

   b. In its second year.
      ❑ Home   ❑ Office   ❑ Factory   ❑ Warehouse
      ❑ Shipping   ❑ Computing   ❑ Other _____

6. Write an estimated total monthly cost for each of these locations.

   a. In your first year.   \$_____
   b. In your second year.   \$_____

7. List every person (by type of duties) who will work for your company (full time, part time, contractor, consultant, etc.) below. Write their duties by type of work (office, sales, programming, etc.), the amount of time they work in a month (part-time, 20 hours per month, full-time, etc.) and what you estimate their monthly costs (or salary) to be. Include yourself with pay.

Person/Duties	Time Estimate	Cost/Year
_____	_____	\$_____
_____	_____	\$_____
_____	_____	\$_____
_____	_____	\$_____
_____	_____	\$_____
_____	_____	\$_____

   a. Total first year costs.   \$_____
   b. Total second year costs.   \$_____

8. List your estimated cost for each item (such as a computer) you need to buy to start your company.

Brief Description of Cost Item   Cost

_____ $_____

_____ $_____

_____ $_____

9. Estimate the costs to market your products or services each year. (For example: publicity, advertising, promotion, commissions, leads program, travel, etc.). Normally these costs are directly related to the actual number or amount of products or services sold. Because the idea is to get a quick estimate, just list each major item that you need to use to market or sell your products or services and estimate a monthly or yearly cost for each item.

Brief Description of Cost Item   Cost

_____ $_____

_____ $_____

_____ $_____

_____ $_____

_____ $_____

   a. Total first year marketing/sales costs. $_____
   b. Total second year marketing/sales costs. $_____

10. List any other overhead, administrative, or other costs you imagine your company needs to pay. Again make a quick estimate for the year.

   a. Total first year administrative costs. $_____
   b. Total second year administrative costs. $_____

11. List any other costs your company must pay to be in business that did not fall into the categories above (manufacturing, raw materials, warehousing, computer lease, programming, long distance, business licenses, telephones, research and development, etc.)

    Brief Description of Cost Item   Cost

    _____ $_____

    _____ $_____

    _____ $_____

    _____ $_____

    _____ $_____

    a. Total first year administrative costs. $_____

    b. Total second year administrative costs. $_____

12. Add up the Total Estimated Costs for each year. First, add all the individual items for each question. If you estimated monthly costs, then multiply your total x the number of months in a year. For the first year, assume you spend one month starting the company.

    a. Total First Year Costs = First year totals for questions 6 + 7 + 8 + 9 + 10 + 11 = $_____

    b. Total Second Year Costs = Second year totals for questions 6 + 7 + 9 + 10 + 11 = $_____

13. Determine your company's yearly income.

    a. In first year 4a – 12a = $_____
    (a positive or a negative number)

    b. In second year 4b – 12b = $_____
    (a positive or a negative number)

14. Add the incomes for your first two years together.

    13a + 13b = $_____

In your opinion:

15. Do you have direct experience, familiarity, or a background with this type of business? ❑ YES ❑ NO

16. Does your company plan to rely on experienced people? ❑ YES ❑ NO

17. Do you have access to, and experience with, these people? ❑ YES ❑ NO

18. If your costs were 10 percent higher and your income 25 percent lower would your business still make a profit? ❑ YES ❑ NO

19. Does your company's profit potential justify its risks? ❑ YES ❑ NO

20. Based on your earlier answers, do you think an investor would make enough money to take this risk? ❑ YES ❑ NO

The Test Results

You can now use the test answers to gain some idea as to how valid your business idea is.

- If you got a positive number for question 14 *AND* you answered YES to questions 15–20, your business idea may have some potential.
- If you got a positive number for question 13 *AND* you answered NO to three or more of questions 15–20, your business concept has potentially serious problems.
- If you got a negative number for question 14, your business concept has financial flaws that must be answered.

How to View Your Results

Use the recommendation from the results as a guideline only. Whether your idea looked potentially reasonable or not, you need to write a business plan. Later chapters will give you information to help you define and estimate your revenues and expenses. The next three chapters present a more formal proof as to whether your company has the potential to make a profit.

The Prefeasibility Test presumed you did not know a lot about your business idea. Its purpose was to get the idea out of your head and onto paper to see if, after writing some of the answers, your vision made sense to you, you still wanted to try it, or if you felt the potential to make a profit.

You have much to gain from reading this book. The more information you bring to your Prefeasibility Test answers, the more you can trust its results. After reading the rest of this book, you may want to go back and test your idea again. The results may surprise you.

4 Research

The Need for Good Business Information

Every part of your business plan must contain solid information. Good business plans have numbers in financial reports that match the text. Revenues, costs, and cash flow balances that lie at the heart of your business plan are based on assumptions.

Every business starts with assumptions. Reasonable, trustworthy assumptions are built from the entrepreneur's *personal, in-depth knowledge* of the subjects, facts, statistics, and events relevant to her business and its products or services, industries, and markets. This knowledge comes from direct experience or—in the case of a growing number of entrepreneurs—from research.

The word *personal* is highlighted to stress the quality of information your company's planning requires. Either you start your company as a former industry insider, find someone who is, or run in-depth research to develop this level of knowledge. If you do not, your company fails. Research is that important.

Your business plan, at a minimum, must contain current, factual information on the

- characteristics of your customers in your market segments, their needs, buying habits, common factors, and likes and dislikes.
- history, size, nature, demand, and trends in your market or markets.
- size, makeup, innovations, trends, and methods of selling, promoting, advertising, distributing, or other operating processes in your industry.
- economic, technologic, regulatory, and other environmental factors that affect your company's chances for success.

Your Vision Affects Your Search

Entrepreneurs continually ask one main question: Where do I find this information? They are overwhelmed by all the information they need. As a result they feel lost when it comes to research and try to shortcut the process. This approach leads to misery, can cost you a lot of money, and is a sure recipe for problems.

The real problem is that most people view their research issues as one big unknown. They either cannot visualize their need for information, or they assume that some company or organization has an *insider* level of knowledge which they cannot hope to find or duplicate. In other words, research needs appear overwhelming. As a result many entrepreneurs overlook the value of a factual basis for their companies.

Leading Edge entrepreneurs understand that business information does not come from one source; it comes from many. The secret to good research is to cut the search process into tiny pieces, where each piece may represent a single fact or a group of closely related facts. Focus on each fact as if it was the only item you need to learn in the whole world. You will be amazed at how fast this method of cutting research problems into bite-sized pieces works.

The Leading Edge Approach to Research

This process of cutting research questions works in four steps:

1. For each piece of information, ask a question; e.g. "Who buys this?" or, "How many dollars worth of maps were sold in the United States last year?" Each question covers *one* piece of information, no more. Write your questions. For example, the market demand in the feasibility study chapters was broken down into individual segments, factors, and relationships—each of which can be measured or estimated. As individual facts, these bits of information are already known, and usually are published.

2. Visualize the answer. What form does it take? Is it one part, or are there several component facts or pieces? How many market segments can you visualize that would need to use maps? Write your thoughts, so that each can become its own question as shown above. You must be able to picture the answer to a question before you can look for it. Otherwise how do you know when you have actually found it? For that matter, how will you judge if it is accurate or meaningful for your purposes if you do not have an idea about it in advance?

3. Once you can picture the form an answer will take, spend a moment thinking who would know this information? Why ask who? Because for many people it is easier to imagine finding a person than finding a fact. Besides, the information for all new businesses initially comes from someone's knowledge, experience, and measurements—so your plan relies on experts if it is to succeed.

4. Once you decide who these experts are, you find them or their published work. Remember that every question you ask has already been answered, and that most of these answers have been published.

Where to Find Information

An easy way to become familiar with your industry is to pay a visit to your local library. You can try a municipal public library, a college or university, or a government, association, or private company library. The staff will be glad to help you use the many source books and directories for all types of businesses.

Every business has a Standard Industrial Classification (SIC) code number. You can find full listings for every imaginable type of business in the SIC code books available in many places including your library. Many source books index their information by SIC code numbers and you have to know yours when dealing with most governmental bodies including government bidding and contracts.

Some information sources are listed below:

- *Thomas Register of Manufacturers*
- *Who's Who in Electronics* (and other industries)
- *Directory of Corporate Affiliations* (parent and subsidiaries)
- *Robert Morris Associates,* a directory found in commercial banks, lists industry costs by SIC code
- *Dun and Bradstreet's Million Dollar Directory* (public and private companies)
- *Moody's Manuals*
- *Standard & Poor's Register of Corporations* (plus other directories)
- *U.S. Industrial Outlook* (good industry overview publication)
- *Ward's Business Directories*
- *Manufacturers Agents National Associations* (lists manufacturer's representatives for every industry)
- *The Encyclopedia of Associations* (breaks down industries by type, lists associations, sizes, costs, locations, publications, and contact information)

- *American Society for Testing Materials (ASTM)* (and other directories of industry standards and testing procedures)
- *Standard Rates and Data Service* (SRDS) (gives publisher's comment, statistics, and advertising rates for all media)
- *United States* government statistics from the Census Bureau and other departments
- *Yellow Pages* for United States cities. Here is a direct overview of the size of any industry in a given area, along with the current telephone numbers of companies
- Trade journals and newspapers, such as *Barron's, The Wall Street Journal,* etc.
- Popular and consumer magazines
- Annual reports to shareholders for local, publicly held companies.
- Most municipal library catalogs now link to the Internet, supplying free business, technical, and consumer database searches.
- Many libraries now offer online or CD access to trademark, patents, and journal databases to the public, usually free, or for a nominal fee.

Government Agencies

The local, state, and federal governments offer as much, or more, specific information as you can find in libraries. Corporate filings and other information are usually a matter of public record, obtainable on microfilm or microfiche, if you are willing to dig for it. Many of these agencies are now putting their records online. Some examples include:

- The U.S. Bureau of the Census, Government Printing Office, or officials in various agencies such as the Securities and Exchange Commission, Department of Agriculture, Department of the Interior, etc.
- If you live in or near a state capital, the Secretary of State, Taxation Department, regulatory agencies, and others can provide superb information, or point you to direct sources.
- Local governments can offer license, tax, title, property, and other records.
- Federal repository libraries. Every state has one. A call to any federal operator can locate the one nearest you. If a statistic exists, they'll have it.
- The U.S. Small Business Administration runs Small Business Development Centers (SBDCs) at community colleges around the US.
- The U.S. SBA SCORE (Service Corps of Retired Executives) program matches retired executives with entrepreneurs.

Industry Insiders

Every industry has many experienced, knowledgeable people willing to talk to you, under the right circumstances:

- Sales representatives have a good "feel" for their segment of an industry or market, but remember to document all your information.
- Every industry has trade associations, so attending national or regional shows or meetings can be very valuable. Or look them up in the *Encyclopedia of Associations*.
- Company Executives or corporate librarians (a favorite of one of the authors).
- Public Information Officers. Large corporations, publicly held companies and government offices have public or investor relations departments with a person responsible for dealing with investors of the public.

Reporters

One excellent source, often overlooked, is to call newspaper, trade journal, magazine, and television reporters directly. Reporters can lead you to insider sources you might never have imagined. They might introduce you to contacts you could not make under other circumstances (see the Approaching Sources section below). They can give you a personal impression of industry contacts, lead you to better sources than you can find alone, or point out trends that have not yet appeared in print.

Reporters are typically very busy, but if you are patient they usually will call you back. Be prepared. Do your background research first, and make sure you are not wasting their time asking for something you can research elsewhere. Tell them why (which story you read) you are calling them. If you form a rapport, or offer them some new information (like your company's exciting new product, or preferably, how some aspect of your industry works), you may get some press later.

Online Databases and the Internet

Online databases often contain information found nowhere else. However, the cost to access, and then search these databases can run to hundreds of dollars an hour. If you choose the wrong database, you may walk away with no usable information for your trouble. We suggest using online databases, via a public library or university, *after* you have done other background research, and checked their appropriateness to your needs.

The Internet can provide a fast and extensive search. If you have never tried it before, we suggest asking your local librarian for instructions. Use Dow-Jones (www.djia.com) for news searches as well as article searches of *The Wall Street Journal* (www.wsj.com), *Barron's* (www.interactive.wsj.com/barrons/), or *Inc.* (www.inconline.com), and many industry-specific publications.

Both authors search the Web routinely—with a caveat! Anybody can represent themselves as anything on the Web, and they often do so. Any information found on the Web is potentially suspect, and should be verified by outside sources, unless you are absolutely convinced that the information source really is whom they claim to be; e.g. the U.S. Securities and Exchange Commission runs Edgar on the Web—a site covering information on publicly traded companies at www.sec.gov.

You will find some additional helpful information on identifying competitive source statistics on this book's Web site at: www.venturea.com.

Approaching Sources

Some personal approaches to research include:

- *Personal Survey.* The best information often comes from a direct look at how other firms operate. Look in the phone book and go visit other firms that are open to the public. Walk in and look around. Do not intrude or be noticeable—just observe. Run an informal survey on your competitions' operations. If promotional literature is available, get copies.
- *Test Results.* Have you run your own?
- *Focus Groups.* These are popular, especially with consumer products, but also depend upon the validity of the test group participants, how the group session was conducted, the line of inquiry, and the make-up of both participant and questioner panels.
- *The Personal Approach.* At times the best answer is to ask someone who is already in the business.

Do your research so that you can ask intelligent questions, understand the answers, and—most important—not waste the interviewee's time. This can lead to many problems, including:

- tipping your hand to potential competitors;
- attempts to mislead, sabotage, or steal what may otherwise be a good idea;
- ethical concerns, particularly if you work in a competing company at the time of contact; and
- becoming discouraged needlessly.

A Leading Edge Example
● ● ● ● ●

Online Mapping Service (OMS)

The owner of Online Mapping Service needs to know the market demand for contour maps like his (see Feasibility Studies, Chapter 5). He grouped his research questions into segments, each of which he solved with grids, or with information:

- At the library he used the *U.S. Statistical Index* to find the total United States and mountain states' populations, plus other breakdowns for ages and consumer habits.

- The *Encyclopedia of Associations* led him to exploration, technology, and recreation trade groups. They led him to Global Positioning Satellite (GPS) terminals, recreational club membership numbers, and geological survey maps sales statistics.

- The managers of two map and outdoor recreation stores gave him product prices and correlation between industrial and personal market segments.

From these sources the owner can decide which market segments benefit from his maps, estimate the number of people in each segment, determine factors affecting people in each segment, and estimate the price to charge for maps. These numbers—and others—justify his financial assumptions.

Summary

To avoid these problems and others, approach different types of sources for in-depth industry, market, product, and technology information by taking the following four steps in order:

1. Search the library for general or industry background, articles, and statistics.
2. Follow up by looking at the annual reports, company Web sites, government statistics, and trade journals.
3. Call suppliers, vendors, sales executives, and trade association officers for information. Obviously, if the information you desire can be answered quickly by local merchants or suppliers, *who have no apparent competitive interest in or relationship with a direct competitor,* just ask them. Just make sure you do not disclose your unique plan, or give them a reason to talk to your competition.

4. Finally, after you have some background information in hand and a good grasp of it, ask the experts. Call those high-level corporate executives, government officials, and university professors to fill in the gaps in your knowledge. Some may be flattered and help you. Others may try to mislead you, which is one way your background information can help.

You might be amazed to discover that by the time you get to the personal sources you wanted to directly question, you already know the answers. If you work for your information, it will prove of immense value in planning your company. Seeing the process removes the mystery. Assuming the information you want exists, knowing the process makes it possible to find it.

If you follow this approach and persist, you will find your answers. If you need more help, contact the authors at venturea.com or at infopr@worldnet.att.net.

5 ·

The Feasibility Study

Now that you have completed a prefeasibility test, the next step is to run a feasibility study. A feasibility study is a special type of business plan, designed to determine if the benefits of a potentially expensive project outweigh its risks.

A feasibility study separates potentially profitable business ideas from all others. Unlike the full business plan, a feasibility study focuses solely on the market demand, sales, revenues, costs, and returns. This makes it faster and easier to test a business idea by homing in on its profitability, without figuring out all the other parts of a functioning company. Like other business plans, the feasibility study has text sections, which explain the assumptions made, the research used, and the results.

A feasibility study concentrates on five critical business factors:

1. The estimated *market size* for your product or service.
2. An estimate of the *market demand* for the product or service.
3. A *sales forecast* based on the demand.
4. A *cost estimate* and an analysis to see if your product or service can be brought to market at a reasonable price.
5. The projected *return on investment* to measure whether the benefits outweigh the risks.

Determining Potential Sales

One of the most important items, when thinking through a business concept, is to demonstrate the overall sales potential for each product or service. The feasibility study approach is an excellent vehicle to determine the entire potential market, and identify all the customers likely to buy your product or service. Determine:

- *Step 1.* Who, within the whole market, is most likely to buy from you? This determines your market segments (covered below).
- *Step 2.* Why are these customers likely to buy from you? Which factors affect each market segment?
- *Step 3.* How many customers, in which niches, within each segment, are likely to buy from you? What is the size of the market?
- *Step 4.* How many customers within each niche is the company able to reach? What percentage of the available market can the company capture?

A feasibility study estimates your potential market size (in dollars), for each product or service. Using the first question, find the market segments. Then:

- Adjust the size of each segment, based on how its related market factors (from step 2) affect it. Usually more than one factor affects a segment's size, e.g., women living in Utah who are between the ages of 23 and 45.
- You can forecast the segment's potential sales volume in dollars (its gross revenues), by multiplying its size (the number of customers in it), by the purchase price for the product or service.
- You can then forecast total projected revenues for each product or service by adding the total revenues from each segment together. This is the sales forecast for a feasibility study.

After you know your total forecast sales, subtract the costs to estimate profits. Normally feasibility studies estimate only the costs directly associated with creating, marketing, selling, and distributing a *manufactured* product. In adapting the feasibility study format as a means to test entrepreneurial ideas, the authors chose to include *all* business expenses, instead of just the direct costs to *manufacture, promote, advertise, distribute, sell* and *administer*, which are normally covered. Listing all costs makes the resulting prediction more accurate for the entrepreneur.

Finally, this chapter uses a single product example (which we do not recommend in starting a company), in an effort to make the concept easier. If you have multiple products or services, which your company should, you merely need to run each separately.

Market Segments

The first step in determining market demand is to define which groups will buy from you. Each group, called a "segment," is made up of people who have common, identifiable characteristics, which make them likely to purchase the same thing. The market for a product or service is found by adding together the many groups (segments) within it.

The most likely customers for any product or service can be grouped by their common needs, which can be measured by:

- Geography: People live, work, or play in a defined location.
- Demography: People are of a particular age, gender, height, income, or other characteristic.
- People most likely to benefit from a product or service.
- Habits or use patterns: People who purchased the same or related products and services in the past, or people determined as *likely* to benefit from a specific product or service.

You can define market segments by looking for one or all of these factors as characteristics of potential customers for your products or services. The good news is that most of these factors have already been measured, and that the measurements are available to literally everyone in the United States who is willing to do the research. Some common characteristics which can be measured or are already published are given below:

Characteristics	**of Consumers**	**of Industrial Customers**
Socioeconomic	Age	Industry
	Sex	Size of Company
	Income	Type of Organization
	Education	Knowledge or Skill Level
Behavioral	Hobbies	Distribution Pattern
	Brands Purchased	Barriers to Customer
	Loyalties	Public vs. Private Co.
Psychological	Personality	Management Style
	Financial Attitude	Industry Payment Patterns

Some market segment examples would include travel magazine subscribers, purchasers of chocolate cookies, women aged 35–45, or civil engineers living in Idaho. Each of these examples shows a market segment measured by common characteristics.

Defining Your Market Segments

A big problem for many business plan writers is defining their target markets. Or, to put it another way, how can you measure your company's potential customers?

A Leading Edge Example   Online Mapping Service (OMS)

Online Mapping Service wants to sell customized, geological contour maps over the Internet. It intends to start business by offering contour maps of the U.S. mountain states. The owner needs to know what factors the most likely customers have in common. He asks:

- What age groups of people are most likely to buy contour maps?

- Where do the buyers live?

- Will they use maps for pleasure, business, travel, or other reasons?

- Do buyers belong to special interest groups?

- Have they bought contour maps, or products that rely on contour maps, before?

Because this company sells products over the Internet, the owner also asks:

- Who uses the Internet?

- How many people own printers with high enough resolution to reproduce readable maps?

You can estimate customers in two ways: taking consumer surveys and extrapolating, or by using the grid method. The grid method is less accurate, but usually more appealing to most entrepreneurs because it uses known information to predict larger—regional, national, or international—markets, in less time, at a lower cost, than conducting surveys.

You can use the grid method to define your market segments in two steps:

1. Ask questions to list common factors or characteristics of your potential customers.
2. Make a two-column grid to decide which parts of each customer group, determined by the questions in step 1, fit into your most likely market segments.

Ask as many questions as possible. Each question helps you think about, and define, the common characteristics of your potential customers. Once you list the factors common to groups of potential customers, you can further define each group by seeing *which parts* of each listed group (your customer niche) represents actual customers. This is where you use the grid.

To estimate the age of his potential customers, the OMS entrepreneur makes a two column-grid from his age question in the boxed example on the previous page. The left column is labeled "Age". The right column is labeled "YES or NO"?

What Ages Represent My Potential Customers?

Age (years)	Yes or No
1–12	N
13–18	Y
19–22	Y
23–35	Y
36–45	Y
46–55	Y
55+	N

The owner groups the ages as shown. Then, in the right hand column, he puts a "Y" next to each age group that he believes or knows is capable of walking, hiking, or traveling in the mountains to the extent that it could use a contour map, and an "N" next to the age groups not representing potential customers..

The process of creating the smaller age segments forces the entrepreneur to carefully think about the groups most likely to buy from him. Later, he can use these age groups, U.S. Census and other data to improve other estimates. He could use a grid to determine each question he lists in an effort to find other market segments.

Market Factors

Each question you asked to establish market segments represents a buying factor, to indicate the likelihood of a particular segment buying from you. As an example, in the age grouping above, more people between the ages of 23 and 35 might buy maps than, say people between the ages of 13 and 18. Or the reverse might be true.

At this point you must either find information, ask for advice, or make an assumption—preferably based on published figures or industry expertise—to determine how much of each segment will buy from you. The type of factor is unique to each entrepreneur and each company. In many cases, one determined factor has an affect on others. Any factor could have a positive or negative influence on other factors that lead to demand. For instance, a younger segment might want a product it cannot afford.

The level and degree of definition for each of these factors, or others factors, depend upon the experience, assumptions, research, knowledge, and judgment of the person making the decisions. Use the table in the Market Segment section, plus a marketing textbook or an adviser's opinion, to develop a list of market factors that affect purchases for your company. An example of how OMS did this will be shown below.

Estimating the Potential Market Size

Once you know your market segments, and you have determined the factors that influence purchase decisions by customers within those segments, you can estimate the market potential for your products or services. Feasibility studies do this using one of three methods:

1. Expert opinions.
2. Research and consumer surveys.
3. Substitute methods.

Most new products and services are either substitutes for or improvements on existing products or services. A substitute is a product or service that replaces one already in existence. If existing markets can be estimated or measured, then potential new markets based on the substitution of one product for another can be calculated from those estimates.

Because each market factor represents a small segment of the group as a whole, you can calculate the effect of each market factor by multiplying or dividing the relevant factors.

A Leading Edge Example, the Potential Market Size for Online Mapping Service

After listing his common characteristics and market factors, the owner of OMS must figure out the demand within his market segments. He does this in five steps:

1. He researches or measures the size of each customer segment.
2. He then determines which other factors affect each segment.
3. He then determines how each factor affects its related segment.
4. Using this information, he adds up the number of people in each segment.
5. Then he adds all the segments together to find his total potential market.

A Leading Edge Example
● ● ● ● ●

Step 1. Research the Potential Market Size for Online Mapping Service

The owner researched his information. Then he estimated or measured (with his research) his common market factors to use these numbers:

- U.S. population: 270,000,000.

- U.S. mountain states' population (people living near the mountains): 40,000,000.

- U.S. Internet users: 55,000,000.

- U.S. laser and inkjet high resolution printer sales: 11,000,000 over the past four years.

- The U.S. Geological Survey: sells 12,500,000 maps, across the country, every year.

- Map distributors and store managers claimed sales for other types of contour maps matched figures for U.S. Geological Survey maps, so the owner assumed 12,500,000 other maps sold per year.

- 250,000 global positioning satellite (GPS) terminals were sold in the previous year.

- 6,000,000 people belong to Scouting, hiking, nature, outdoor. and environment groups and/or buy hunting licenses in the mountain states each year.

Step 2. Determine the Market Factor Relationships

- The owner uses multiplication or division to determine the relationships between various market factors. For example:

- Of 270,000,000 U.S. citizens, 40,000,000 live in mountain states. 40 million/270 million = 14.8% of the U.S. population lives in mountain states.

- 55,000,000 people out of 270,000,000 use the Internet. 55 million/270 million = 20.4% of all potential map buyers can make online purchases from his Web-based company.

- Assuming all Web users have access to a printer, then 11 million printers/55 million Internet users = 20% of Internet users have printers with sufficient resolution.

- The age group distribution of Internet users places 80% between the ages of 18 and 55.

- Based on conversations with mining, exploration, outdoor management and related companies, and government agencies, the owner assumes that for every GPS terminal sold, four contour maps are purchased per year.

- After talking to several outdoor associations and groups, the owner chose two maps sold per member per year as reasonable.

Step 3. Estimate the Market Size

The owner decides to estimate the market based on past use. He knows or estimates:

   12 million U.S. Geological Survey (USGS) maps sold per year.
+ 12 million other contour maps sold (= USGS purchases).
+ 12 million interest group sales (6,000,000 × 2 maps each per year).
+ 1 million GPS terminals (250,000 × 4 maps each per year for 1 year).
= 37 million maps per year sold. This is his Total Market Size.

The Market Demand

The total Market Demand for *all* your products or services is determined by multiplying the number of people in each defined market segment times the price paid for the product or service in that segment.

A Leading Edge Example
● ● ● ● ●

The Market Demand for All Contour Maps

The number of maps sold × the average sale price per map = the Potential Market.

- On average, USGS maps sold for $4.75 in 1998.

- Other company's contour maps sold at an average price of $8.95.

Store managers and government sales figures showed that USGS maps sales roughly matched the totals from all similar types of maps. The owner of OMS decided to take the average price between retail and USGS contour maps as examples for what the market would pay for his maps.

He then estimated the Potential Market for all contour maps as:

$$= \frac{\$(4.75 + 8.95)}{2} = \frac{\$13.70}{2} = \$6.85/\text{map}$$
$$\times 37{,}000{,}000 \text{ maps per year}$$
$$= \$253{,}450{,}000 \text{ per year}$$

If the OMS owner decides to include other factors, or use more carefully drawn projections or assumptions, this Potential Market will change.

Forecasting Sales

You can forecast sales based on the amount of the market you expect to reach, assuming your price is acceptable to the market. In Chapter 12, The Marketing Strategy, you will learn more about differentiating, publicizing, promoting, pricing, and selling products or services. In a feasibility study, you *assume* these factors will match the industry norms.

Sales typically are forecast by:

1. Multiplying the company's market factors (determined earlier) by the Total Market Demand.
2. To forecast likely sales, and keep sales forecasts reasonable, multiply the Total Potential Sales Forecast by a factor that represents the company's ability to reach a smaller portion of the whole market. This is shown in the following boxed example.

A Leading Edge Example
● ● ● ● ●

Step 4. Forecasting Potential Sales for OMS Market Segment

Online Mapping Service's owner must determine how each segment of his $253,450,000 potential market demand can be served by his company. He multiplies his Market Factors together:

14.8% of the US population lives in the right area
$\times$ 20.3% of these people have Internet access
$\times$ 20.0% of these people have the right printer
$\underline{\times 80.0\%}$ of this number are the correct age
$=$ $.148 \times .203 \times .20 \times .80 = .004807$

The Total Market $\times$ Market Factors = Total Potential Sales

$= \$253,450,000 \times 0.004807 = \$1,218,34$ per year.

Step 5. Forecasting Potential Sales for OMS Market Share

To forecast his annual sales, OMS's owner multiplies his total potential sales from all segments by the part of the market he believes his company can reach. As a newly defined, wide open, Internet-based niche, the owner estimates he can reach 25 percent of his potential niche in the first year.

Total Potential Sales $\times$ Estimated Market Reach =
Company Sales Forecast

$= \$1,218,334 \times 0.25 = \$304,584.$

The owner knows OMS cannot reach 100 percent of its market. Despite his short-term technology edge, which he believes will appeal to customers, and market research that found no similar competitor, he understands that no company is 100 percent effective. He assumes that with serious effort, good Web publicity, a traditional media blitz, excellent customer service, very hard work, and some luck—his company can reach one out of four potential buyers. To project future sales, the owner of OMS would have to look at changes in different market factors.

This estimation of market reach is one of the biggest downfalls we see in revenue projections. No matter who you think will buy from you, the number is probably less—much less.

Costs

A feasibility study attempts to predict and measure costs. Because new companies carry a high financial risk, all of its costs are compared to its potential sales. Costs generally fall into certain categories. The four most common costs associated with these categories are:

1. Start-Up Costs

Financing Expenses	Equipment and Supplies	Failures, Mistakes, and Waste
Consultants	Legal Fees	Facilities
Training	Deposits	Other

2. Manufacturing or Direct Expenses

Material	Factory Rent	Utilities
Labor	Maintenance	Manufacturing Office Space
Supervision	Toolroom	Insurance

3. Sales and Marketing Expenses

Salaries	Travel	Fulfillment
Commissions	Shipping	Other
Advertising	Promotions	

4. General and Administrative Expenses

Leased Facilities	Utilities	Insurance
Leased Equipment	Personnel	Other
Supplies	Depreciation	

Analyzing Costs

Costs are checked either by using a Sensitivity Analysis or a Technical Analysis. A *Sensitivity Analysis* measures how a change in one cost component in a manufacturing process could effect the ultimate product price or profitability of the process (service providers are discussed later). Cost sensitivity is better covered in a marketing text than here.

A *Technical Analysis* asks questions to determine the main cost areas. You can figure out your costs based on the factors shown for the four areas listed directly above, or from the main processes that make up your company's activities.

In either case, to analyze costs, you:

1. Imagine each process in the company.
2. Determine all the procedures or parts within each process.
3. List the persons, tasks, or items that make up each procedure or process.
4. Place a cost next to each of these items.
5. Total all the costs.
6. Categorize each type of cost based on the four types (Start-Up, Manufacturing or Direct Sales and Marketing, and General and Administrative) shown on the previous page.
7. Finally, you multiply each set of costs by the number of months in which the cost is incurred.

Technical Cost Analysis Questions

By nature most business start-ups have no operating history and do not involve manufacturing expenses. As a result most Leading Edge entrepreneurs will be likely to use a *Technical Analysis* to determine costs. The questions below can help with this process:

1. Can you describe the entire process to create and deliver each of your products or services to their intended markets?   ❑ YES   ❑ NO

    a. Will each process or service work as you envision it?
    b. Can the product be built?
    c. Can the service be delivered?
    d. Is there a history of similar products or services being presented by this method?
    e. Is a similar process in use today, or will your company depart from what has gone before?

2. Are the appropriate personnel, resources, tools,
   and materials on hand?   ❏ YES   ❏ NO

   a. Do you know all the information you need to know, or have
      you worked out the entire concept for your company?
   b. Are there special information, materials, resources, or facilities
      critical to your company which you do not have at present?
   c. Do you have a tangible or measurable method to acquire these
      resources?
   d. Have you determined the cost to acquire these resources?
   e. Is there any part you have not checked or analyzed?

3. Will your business run all of its own processes,
   or does it rely on outside contractors or
   companies for fulfillment?   ❏ YES   ❏ NO

   a. Are these contractors or companies local?
   b. Do they have experience in fulfilling your desired process?
   c. Do you have experience in managing procedures similar to
      what you will have them do?
   d. Have you gotten estimates for the cost for their services?
   e. Do these costs generally match those within the industry?
   f. If any contractor or company fails, will your company remain
      in business?

4. Will your company require financing?   ❏ YES   ❏ NO

   a. Will you need capital to start?
   b. Will you need working capital or reserves?
   c. Have you ever managed large sums of money before?
   d. Do you have someone who can help with this process?
   e. Is this person experienced in managing money?

5. Do you personally have the knowledge or
   experience to manage all of your company's
   processes and procedures?   ❏ YES   ❏ NO

   a. Have you located the necessary expertise or personnel?
   b. Have you determined how many people you need?
   c. Have you determined the cost of these people?
   d. Will they be available to your company when you need them?
   e. Can you name these people?

6. Have you made a schedule or timetable to develop each product or service you intend to bring to market?　　　　❑ YES　❑ NO

   a. Did you compare your schedule to others within the industry?
   b. Does it call for faster deliveries, lower costs, or vary in other ways from present industry or market standards?

7. Does the company require a high level of costs for startup?　　　　❑ YES　❑ NO

   a. Does your company need an office, a manufacturing or a storage facility, or other real estate?
   b. Do you need to be in a special location?
   c. Have you determined the price for this location?
   d. Is this location available?

8. Does your company require expensive equipment?　　　　❑ YES　❑ NO

   a. Is this equipment necessary before you start operations?
   b. Will you need to add equipment later?
   c. Is this equipment necessary to produce your primary product or service?, or
   d. Is this equipment necessary for a supporting process?
   e. Is this equipment presently available?
   f. Have you determined its price?

An Example of Costs: Online Mapping Service

The owner of OMS places his primary costs into a spreadsheet. He decides to run the company from a home office. He needs several major expense items:

- Custom software programming to customize maps and allow people to see them in advance, without being able to take them without paying for them.
- A leased computer server, with experts to run it, to store his software, data, and Web site. A company computer, scanner, and printer with fax/modem capabilities, and Internet service.
- High bandwidth (data volume) telephone lines into the Internet, plus backup lines.
- Access to map information, and an employee to scan it into the system.

- A secure merchant bank account to handle online credit card transactions.
- An attorney to ensure he has no copyright problems.

He talks to a friend who writes software programs. The friend claims it will take 40 hours to write the program he needs. Because every programmer underestimates costs and deliveries, the owner budgets for 80 hours, twice the estimate. At $60/hour his initial programming cost is $4,800. He estimates startup costs:

Start-Up Costs

Personal expenses for one month	$ 3,000
Computer server lease deposit	$ 400
Outside software programming	$ 4,800
Domain names registration	$ 140
Phone lease deposit	$ 400 For phone lines
Supplies	$ 200
Publicity/Advertising	$ 3,000
Legal fees	$ 500 For incorporation
Technical Writer	$ 3,500
Web site development	$ 3,000
Printed materials/Brochures	$ 850
Graphics	$ 1,200
Insurance	$ 275
Other	$ 650
	$21,915

Product Expenses at Start-up

U.S. Geological Survey Maps on CD	$ 2,856
Licensing fees for other mapping service	$ 8,000 (Estimated)
Licensing attorney	$ 3,500
Global Positioning Software	$ 595
Global Positioning Scanner	$ 459 For testing purposes
OCR (optical character recognition) software	$ 550
Top-of-the-line scanner	$ 1,700
CAD (computer aided design) software	$ 600
Adobe Photoshop™ (graphics) software	$ 579
Other scanning software	$ 575
Software training	$ 600 (Estimated)

Contract labor to scan maps for two months.	$ 5,800 (Estimated)
Cost of testing maps (by driving in state)	$ 200 (1 week; expenses)
Other Travel (airfare, hotel/meals)	$ 1,800 (Estimated)
Long distance telephone costs	$ 200
Subtotal	$28,014
Other product expenses @ 10%	$ 2,801
Subtotal	$30,815

Product Expenses (Annual)

Merchant account (credit card charges) @3.5% of gross sales	$10,660
Losses/Problems/Returns @1.5% of gross sales	$ 4,569
Subtotal	$15,229

As this book was written, typical charges against purchases for Internet, credit card services appeared to average 3.5 percent. Normally, new companies use a figure of 0.5 percent to 1.0 percent to calculate losses and returns. Because OMS operates in a new medium where customers cannot actually see the business with which they interact, the owner estimate his losses at 1.5 percent.

Sales and Marketing Expenses (Monthly)

Publicity/Advertising	$ 1,400
Newswire services	$ 550
Print/other advertising	$ 2,000
Press releases/other writing	$ 800
	$ 4,750
Other expenses @ 10 %	$ 475
	$ 5,225

Salaries and Personnel Costs (Monthly)

Personal salary	$ 3,000
Benefits @ 35%	$ 1,050
Other/Contract labor	$ 1,500
	$ 5,550

General and Administrative Expenses (Monthly)

Computer server lease	$ 400	Includes firewall/ secure commerce server
Utilities	$ 80	
Insurance	$ 75	
Liability insurance	$ 65	In case people get lost and sue.
High speed telephone access	$ 126	
Additional programming	$ 400	/mo. (estimated)
Accounting/Tax service	$ 900	
Printing	$ 125	
Postage/Shipping	$ 85	
Bank account	$ 45	
Other supplies	$ 150	
	$ 2,451	
Other (Contingent @ 10 %)	$ 245	
	$ 2,696	

Based on his primary costs the owner is looking at an annual cost to operate:

One-Time Costs	
Start-up	$21,915
Product start-up	$30,815
Product expense (Annual)	$15,229
	$67,959
Monthly Costs	
Sales and marketing	$ 5,225
Salaries	$ 5,550
General and administrative	$ 2,696
	$13,471 per month × 11 months in first year = $148,181

Total first year expenses = $67,959 + $148,181 = $216,140

Gross Revenues minus expenses equals the Gross Margin.

Gross Revenues	$304,583	(From the sales forecast)
– Expenses	–216,140	(From above)
= Gross Margin of	$ 88,443	

The company's pro forma statement for this feasibility study did not take financing charges or taxes into account. It estimated some expenses and assumed percentages of annual sales as costs for other expense items. In his estimates the owner added 10% to each expense category.

If, to be conservative, he cut his earnings estimate by 25 percent, then

Gross Revenues $304,583 × 0.75 = $228,437
– Expenses   –216,140
= Gross Margin of $ 12,297
The company projects a profit.

Return on Investment

The real question answered by all feasibility studies is: Does the return on investment justify the investment risk? The owner needs $67,000 in startup expenses (shown above), to which he adds a 10 percent reserve to equal $75,000. He calculates his return on investment as:

$$\text{Return on Investment (ROI)} = \frac{\text{Net Profit}}{\text{Investment}}$$

$$\text{ROI} = \frac{\$(304,583 - 216,140)}{\$75,000} = \frac{\$88,443}{\$75,000} = 1.18$$

Online Mapping is calculated to return the entire risk amount, plus eighteen percent in the first year. If the company makes 25 percent less than the projected $304,000, then:

$$\text{ROI} = \frac{(\$304,583 \times 0.75) - \$216,140}{\$75,000} = \frac{\$228,437 - \$216,140}{\$75,000} = \frac{\$12,297}{\$75,000} = 0.163$$

After lowering its income estimates, the company still shows a net positive return of 16 percent in its f4irst year. All feasibility studies look for positive ROI number during the period under review, which in this case is one year. Because 16 percent is a positive number, the feasibility study would conclude that the financial risk to start the company is worth taking.

Writing the Feasibility Study Text

A feasibility study may include 10 to 25 pages of narrative text. The text runs in sections that cover:

- An Executive Summary
- Preliminary Assumptions
- The Potential Market

- Revenues
- Costs
- Return on Investment
- Results and Conclusions
- Information Sources

The purpose of the text is to outline the reasons for doing the study and to define the study methods, information, and assumptions used, and tell why. Based on the results, the study will either recommend, or not recommend, running the project or new company.

By its nature, the feasibility study can be changed many times to reflect different market or cost factors. The more accurate the information and the assumptions, the more the recommendations can be trusted. One way to improve the study is to run sales and cost estimates in a manner similar to the pro formas shown later in this book.

A brief note: Online Mapping Service's feasibility study is shown as a sample business plan in the Appendix. It includes a one year, month-by-month, pro forma estimate of revenues. The original pro forma estimate of revenues came out higher than the revenues shown using the assumptions in this chapter. As a result, the lower numbers derived in this chapter's example were used.

Summary

A feasibility study attempts to justify the projected revenue stream from a product or service without going into all the details necessary to write a full business plan. This look at markets, revenues, cost factors, and returns is a good way to indicate if your business concept has profit potential.

This direct look at assumptions, markets, costs, and returns enables the entrepreneur to determine if the money making aspects of the business make sense *before* undertaking the long term, but obviously important considerations for the actual personnel, locations, sources of supply or products, and other business planning processes. If the feasibility study forecasts a negative return on investment, the entrepreneur can either go back and improve the research, costs, or other assumptions directly, or decide to abandon the project—without having to put in the time to determine other considerations needed for a successful company.

As you research and write the feasibility study, facts about running your venture will become clearer. As you gain understanding and clarity, you can revise your concept and start writing the business plan, knowing in advance that your venture has a reasonable chance to make a profit.

6 ·

Testing Reality

Bringing a product or service to market is an intricate process that takes time, money, resources, and discipline. The marketing process for a new product or service, combined with the complexity of starting a company, may call for personal sacrifice.

Before going through this process, you must test reality. This chapter introduces three management tools used by corporations to help them determine, when they enter new markets, which factors will affect them most and what strategies to develop.

These tools are: the GAP Analysis, the SWOT Test, and the Key Success Factors. They can help you draw a better picture of your company, its strengths, weaknesses, and strategies.

- A GAP Analysis defines where your company is today; where it is to go in the future; and the gap between them. A GAP Analysis uses the formal question-and-answer process to pinpoint a company's objectives, milestones and goals, and the steps—the processes, functions, and activities—needed to reach its goals and match your vision.
- The SWOT Test measures your company's internal *Strengths* and *Weaknesses* in comparison to its industry. It lists the *Opportunities* and *Threats* the industry faces from its external environment. Knowing each factor helps you set long-term strategies.
- The Key Success Factors are essential items that your company *must* address or take advantage of to compete successfully.

It is much easier to learn from testing than it is to learn from mistakes. These tools can help you gain a better idea of where your company stands within its industry environment. Their main value comes in defining the factors and developing strategies to deal with them, something few new, or small, companies attempt. This set of tools can give the Leading Edge entrepreneur vital information to gain a competitive edge.

The Big Picture—The GAP Analysis

Companies start from dreams. Although dreams are pleasant, they are, by nature, too vague to define and describe the parts and details necessary to run a company. Entrepreneurs usually know some parts of their business—their products or services—much better than others, like their industry or markets. These entrepreneurs frequently hold a fixed image of their company's future—such as the amount of money it will make—without a clear grasp of the steps it takes to make this money.

The GAP Analysis finds and fills in missing information about your company's growth process. It lists the activities, objectives, milestones, and goals for your company, based on your personal view and knowledge. Use the following four steps:

1. Draw a picture of how your company operates all of its processes at start-up.
2. Draw a picture of how your company will operate its processes at some future point.
3. Compare your two pictures to see what is missing in between them. The difference between these two pictures is the "GAP," the objectives and milestones your company must accomplish to reach its goals. You define GAP objectives by either working forward from the present, or backward from the future.
4. After defining GAP objectives and milestones, you can then determine the activities (the specific tasks) necessary to accomplish them.

The result is a picture, a road map, of your company, running from the present to the future. Your GAP road map shows you where to go, what to accomplish, and *which activities or events to ignore or embrace* for your company to be successful.

The real value of the GAP Analysis is in making entrepreneurs and executives ask questions and write descriptions showing how the company does—and will—work. It may help to have a trusted adviser "brainstorm" the GAP questions with you.

Write your answers and statements, then save them. When it comes time to review your company in the future, your GAP Analysis answers can serve as a memory of your vision.

The GAP Analysis Statements

Most companies have two or three functions or processes that are central to its existence, separate from marketing and sales. Detailing these processes is done later in the book, but for the moment, just try to list them to get an idea of what each covers.

The steps below cover your company's sales, administrative, and other functions. These functions, become outline headings that show the steps (the processes) to fulfill each function. The functions and processes draw a picture of *how* your company will operate after you open your doors for business.

Step 1. Draw a picture of your company today.

1. Describe your company's sales goals for the month you actually start the company (or for the first month you intend to make sales). How many products or services will your company sell— each day, each week, or each month? What price will your company charge for each? Where does the sale take place? Describe the sales process?

2. List every *direct* function your company must perform to sell each product or service. Retail, distribution, wholesale, manufacturing, and service companies have many processes that go into a sale. This list can vary depending on the type of company and how it makes money. The idea is to make sure you list *all* the related business functions for your company.

3. List the processes that make up each function shown in the statement above. Each of the functions above can have many parts. The raw materials come from many places, each of which was chosen for specific reasons. If you sell a service, its marketing processes may include: research to define potential customer groups, publicity to let each group know about your service, promotion to each group, direct or indirect sales calls, etc. You may end up with five to eight steps for each process.

4. List the primary processes in statement 3 that your company will do in-house.

5. Describe how each primary process touches your product or service. This description makes assumptions. For example, to market your service may require publicity. Your publicity effort *assumes* that sending letters, brochures, or articles to a defined organization leads to some potential sales contacts. The idea is to define the steps in the process: (a) send letters, (b) make sales contacts, (c) make sales calls, and (d) close sales.

6. Fill in the numbers for each assumption made in statement 5. This makes it possible for you to anticipate *how many* times each item takes place in any function, or step within it. That gives you a clear idea of the process, who will undertake it, and what must be done. You may find as you fill in your assumptions that new issues come forward, or that some of your listed steps or processes change. Do not worry. Each item completed now is either money in the bank, or it may show potential problems to be overcome if you wish to start—or grow—your company.

7. Now answer questions 1 through 6 for the other processes in your company. These include: How will you run the company? Who works with you—full time, part-time, as a consultant, or as an adviser? How will you find suppliers, vendors, and sales outlets? Where will you obtain the money to finance these operations?

A Leading Edge Example
● ● ● ● ●

Luminous Paint Products, Inc.

Luminous Paint Products manufactures and distributes specialty coatings for fiberglass, concrete, and steel surfaces. It uses an outside firm to blend raw materials into its coatings. How many processes go into each Luminous sale? Nine. The company must:

1. Buy raw materials, chemicals, dyes, containers, labels, and other items.

2. Ship these materials to its warehouse.

3. Move the raw materials to the custom paint blending factory.

4. Have the factory manufacture coatings from them.

5. Store the products.

6. Sell the products.

7. Ship the products to customers.

8. Take payment on each transaction.

9. Service other needs from each customer.

Step 2. How do you view your company's future?

Now it is time to create a possible future for your company. Many people see a certain level of sales at some unknown point; others try to imagine sales one or two years down the road. Still others imagine a certain level of income, or a certain lifestyle.

You need uncontaminated information for the second step of GAP. It is important that as you determine the descriptions in part two of the GAP Analysis, you do *not* read—or otherwise compare—the statements you reach to those you obtained in part one.

1. Pick a point in the future and describe your company's sales using the first statement in Step 1.
2. Go back through the other items from Step 1 to describe the underlying functions and activities necessary to reach the company's future shown in question 1, Step 2.

For example, Luminous Paints set a goal to sell $25,000 worth of paint—approximately 1,000 gallons per month—in its first year. This level of activity means the company must administer, handle, and distribute so many items that it needs a full-time employee to track the paint.

As you identify and relate each function in your company's picture, your knowledge of that function, and what it takes to accomplish it, grows. By the end of Step 2, you will know how your company will look and operate in the future, who will work there, and under what conditions.

Step 3. Analyze the GAP between the present and the future.

This is where you fill in the blanks between the present and the future.

1. Review your Step 1 notes on your company's functions, processes, goals, milestones, activities and any figures in your assumptions. Do the same for your future "picture."
2. Mark every area with a noticeable difference (gap) between your company's present and future objectives and goals.
3. For each function or process where the underlying goals, activities, or numbers changed noticeably, determine a reasonable step—or group of steps—to get from one to the other. You can work forward from the present or backward from the future, as long as the added steps fill the gaps.

Some areas to watch include places where:

- You add products or services, or change the approach to your industry or market.
- You add or change operating procedures or personnel to accomplish the next step.
- You alter the process by which a function occur, to improve its outcome.

For example, Computer Training Services teaches people how to use Microsoft™ software products. In its first months, the owner, intends to teach most classes himself, with one part-time teacher. As the number of students and courses grows, CTS moves the second teacher from part-time to full-time, and adds a third teacher. Each change leads to others.

4. Some questions to ask when these functions change include:
    - Who will do the work that must be accomplished at this point?
    - What level of activity (how many items) must be completed to reach these intermediate goals in a reasonable manner?
    - Where does this activity take place?
    - How much will it cost in human resources, money, time, and other resources?
    - Finally, ask yourself, does this intermediate step fit in this place? Is it complete?

5. Repeat items 3 and 4 until you can "see" the activities to accomplish all the milestones and objectives from your starting image to the future image of your company.

This is the heart of the GAP Analysis. Now you either have a picture of the activities, goals, and milestones to move your company along its path, or a good idea of the research you need to draw your picture.

Answering the GAP Analysis questions should give you a new understanding of how your company will work. The completed GAP Analysis can help you build your operations plan as it indicates what areas need work.

The SWOT Analysis

The SWOT Analysis points out your company's *S*trengths, *W*eaknesses, *O*pportunities, and *T*hreats. Your internal strengths are based on how your company stacks up against its competitors. Opportunities and threats are those faced by your industry as a whole. The more you know about your industry and market, the better your answers. A SWOT Analysis takes four steps:

1. Determine your company's strengths and weaknesses in its industry.

2. Determine the opportunities and threats facing your company's industry.
3. Develop strategies to take advantage of the opportunities or meet the threats.
4. Discuss them with your business advisers to develop strategies

It is important to note that All SWOT factors are based on a *comparison* with your competition. If your company has superior management in an industry that generally offers superior management, this is *NOT* a strength. Recognizing and understanding SWOT factors helps business managers set up realistic strategy options.

The SWOT Analysis creates a profile of your company, which you can then discuss with your advisers. This profile lets you go back over your previously developed information to see if it should be improved in light of your findings, and to make sure it is reasonable for you to start a company.

Running the SWOT Analysis

Step 1. Identify your company's strengths or weaknesses.

Your strengths and weaknesses are based on how your company differs from its competitors. You may only find one or two strengths and several weaknesses, but do not worry. Each company is different.

- A *Strength* is a unique competence that gives your company a competitive advantage in its marketplace. It can be a skill, resource, technology, or other advantage that your company has which its competitors lack.
- A *Weakness* is a lack of or deficiency in skills, resources or capabilities that seriously hurts your company's ability to perform, compared to what your competitors possess. Sources of weaknesses can include lack of financial resources, knowledge, experience, marketing skills, product awareness, or management capabilities.

Compare your company to its competitors by building a two-column grid.

1. List your company in the top, right hand cell.
2. Down the left side, list the factors or qualities that your background or industry research determined to be important.

3. Then place an "X" in each cell where your company appears to have a strength.
4. Leave the grid cells blank where your company has a weakness.
5. Ask how, or if, your company differs from its market or industry in each of those areas.

If you did a good job of researching your industry, the common factors for your industry will appear within it. Use those factors, or the ones that appear relevant from the list below, when you draw your grid.

The needs you determined from the GAP Analysis also can represent industry or market factors. Ask yourself, "Which factors would an investor think are important?" The goal is to be thorough in assessing competitive factors.

A List of Industry Factors

Marketing.

- Width and depth of product/service line(s)
- Effective sales organization or processes
- Efficiency, effectiveness, and imagination of sales publicity, advertising, and promotion
- Pricing strategy and flexibility
- Ability to gather important market information
- Potential market share or segment share based on measured information
- Channels of distribution
- After-sale customer relations, service, and follow-up
- Goodwill, recognition, brand loyalty, or references.

Financial.

- Cost of market entry
- Barriers to market entry
- Ability to raise capital
- Cost of capital relative to competitors and industry
- Effective cost control, and the ability to reduce costs
- Financial size within your defined market segments

General or technical operations.

- Access to new technology or innovation advantage
- Quality of underlying technology (often essential to new companies)
- Availability of raw materials and products (for product companies)
- Availability of project time or subcontractors time (for service companies)
- Location, layout, and utility of facilities (for wholesale, retail, and distribution companies)
- Inventory control system or effective distribution (for product or service companies)
- Economies of scale

Your list can include management or other factors, but this list will give you some idea of what you are after.

Step 2. Determine the opportunities and threats facing your industry.

(We changed the definition of "industry" for this step, to match its results with the needs of startup company entrepreneurs. Instead of competing against the giants of industry, which normally occurs in SWOT, our version of Step 2 involves your direct or local competition.)

Just as a new company faces internal challenges, its industry also faces similar issues. Normally, for SWOT, these include:

- *Opportunities* are major positive events or situations in an industry's environment, such as: a new technology, a newly defined market segment, improved supplier or buyer relationships, or other positive events from which your company—unlike its competitors—benefits.
- *Threats* are major unfavorable factors in your industry's external environment. These factors can involve: new competitors, one competitor's technological advances, lower cost structures, increased bargaining power, recognition or better vendor or supplier relationships by competitors, slowing market growth or decay, or new regulations, which may hurt your company.

Your direct, local, or regional competitors have defined methods (standards) of doing business. As you run your company, and presumably increase in size, you can change your definition of the competition as it becomes appropriate.

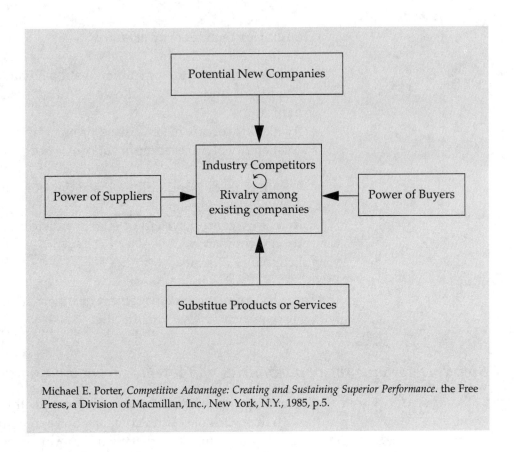

Michael E. Porter, *Competitive Advantage: Creating and Sustaining Superior Performance*. the Free Press, a Division of Macmillan, Inc., New York, N.Y., 1985, p.5.

Industry Competitive Forces

In any industry, the nature of the competition depends on the interaction of the five forces shown above, originally identified by Michael E. Porter.

1. Define your industry's general environment (how your direct competition competes) in the center box.
2. Ask how the factors in each surrounding box, affects your industry? For example:
   - What is the bargaining power of the buyers? If, for example, one buyer can become so large that it can dictate terms to your industry, how will your company handle that threat? What strategy or policy will it adopt?
   - What is the threat of a new (substitute) product or service entering the market? Can your existing product or service be replaced?
   - What is the bargaining power of the suppliers?

- What is the threat of new companies entering the industry?
3. Determine which industry threats and opportunities affect your company.

A Leading Edge Example
• • • • •

Competitive Strategies for Construction Delivery Corporation (CDC)

CDC developed an innovative "virtual" blueprint room service for contractors on the Internet. It faces threats from:

- Potential entrants—blueprint companies moving onto the Internet

- Other (substitute) online software products created by Web-based companies

The company establishes strategies to ensure its software works better than the competition, and to gain industry-wide recognition *before* competitors arrive.

As market recognition grows, CDS can become a standard location to find blueprints for new projects, which represents a potential growth market.

Step 3. Analyze the nature of your company's strategy to meet each opportunity or threat.

Opportunities come from situations like:

- A company has an advantage in terms of supply, distribution, etc.
- Creating a new, better, product line (one way new companies often compete)
- Hiring expertise
- Raising capital, other financial expertise

Threats come from situations like:

- Losing a technological edge
- A new industry entrant
- Government regulations, or new processes prescribed by the industry
- Tightening credit or capital problems
- Quickly changing innovation or technology

For a new company dependent on technology innovation or operating on the Internet with virtual products or services, the threats from new entrant companies or new product entries can be very high.

Step 4. Discuss the results with your advisers.

Because most new companies are by nature aggressive, you should consider the industry opportunities and threats as part of a long term strategy *after* you have established a solid foothold. The purpose in having you explore this step is to make you aware of your industry, because like a boat in the sea, your company's fortunes are affected by the industry's rise and fall and the changes in its currents.

Determining Key Success Factors

All companies must be able to take advantage of their industry's or market's key success factors if they are to be successful. To determine your Key Success Factors:

1. Survey potential (or existing) customers and ask them what companies they believe compete with you? If possible, ask for 3 large, 3 medium, and 3 small companies.
2. Either run the survey yourself by walking into or asking people outside competitor establishments, or call them on the phone.
   - If you call potential customers on the phone, ask them if they ever used these companies' products or services?
   - If they did, ask them what they liked or remembered, based on the survey questions shown in Chapter 12, The Marketing Strategy.
3. Gather the brochures, literature, press releases, and news stories for these companies.
4. Based on what you read and hear, make a list of your competitors' features, benefits, and qualities.
5. Build a chart placing each competitor's name along the top, and listing all qualities down the left side (as shown in the first SWOT step, earlier in this chapter).
6. Place an "X" in each cell where a competitor has a quality, benefit, or feature.
7. Find the rows which have the most filled-in cells. The two to four cells with the most Xs represent the most likely key success factors.
8. Ask yourself "What can or must my company do about this identified factor?" If you can meet or fulfill it, it is a potential opportunity. If not, then you must rethink your approach to the business.

A Leading Edge Example
● ● ● ● ●

Luminous Paint's Industry Strategies

Luminous Paint has a technological edge in the form of longer lasting, more easily applied coatings, which gives it a competitive advantage over other's in the paint industry.

- It does not have in-house manufacturing capacity, which is basic to the business. It lacks distribution beyond its region, a key component in the paint industry.

- If the owner cannot find a way to overcome these issues he cannot succeed in the long term.

He sets a strategy to dominate in marginal, local areas, to avoid recognition as he builds inventory and capital and awaits test results which permit wider industry competition. His internal funding strategy (shown as a business plan example in the Appendix) limits his potential losses to no more than the revenues the company gained from the owner's direct sales.

Ask Your Advisers

Ask your advisers, people with recognized knowledge or expertise within your industry or markets, for their opinions as to which factors they feel are key to success in your chosen industries or markets.

1. Discuss with your advisers each success factor in your industry or market.
2. Devise a strategy for how your company can compete.

The Million Dollar Question: Can My Company Succeed?

Every industry has its own ways of doing business. The standard methods cover factors like the level of financing, product innovation, product life cycles, quality of management, cost of goods sold, sales methods, market penetration and distribution patterns, company size or sales volume, and many others.

Every industry factor, strength, weakness, opportunity, and threat is important, but some are more important than others. To operate in an industry over time, your company must meet or exceed every *key success factor.* By carefully researching and analyzing your competitors' strengths and weaknesses, and the unmet needs within their markets, you can find the most important factors for your company's success.

Listen closely to how your advisers view your answers to GAP, SWOT and the Key Success Factors. There should be some disagreement, and plenty of discussion. If they agree with every point you present, you have the wrong advisers. Advisers should offer different views and a higher level of information.

If your advisers disagree with your conclusions, pay close attention to the solutions they present to overcome the problems they see. Listen carefully to their opinions on how to exploit your company's potential advantages. Remember these results are not final; they merely represent information from which to build a company strategy.

The GAP Analysis and SWOT Test give you an idea of what you need to accomplish and what is most important if you are to succeed in business. Your goal is to answer three questions. They are:

1. Should you formulate and write a plan to finance and operate your company?
2. Can you do this at a profit, with a reasonable level of risk?
3. Does your company have the potential to repay your investors—whether it is yourself, your family or associates, financial angels, venture capitalists, or bankers?

If you answered yes to all three questions, read on in the next section, knowing you had good teachers—your competitors and industry experts. If not, consider yourself lucky that reality testing saved you time, money, and grief.

7

Writing a Leading Edge Business Plan

Incorporate Nine Guiding Principles into Your Leading Edge Plan

Here are the nine general guidelines explaining the basic elements of a Leading Edge business plan. These should be helpful in writing any type business plan, no matter to whom it is directed.

1. *Make it easy to read.* To win the competition for financing dollars today, your plan must be well formatted and easily understood. Your introductory statement summarizing your operation is one of the most important sections; it must capture the readers' attention and motivate them to read the balance of your plan. Caution: If they need a dictionary at their side in order to read, they'll stop. Include a glossary if you must use a lot of technical words.

2. *Your approach should be market-driven, not product-driven.* Especially, if you want those magic money doors to open, you must understand that investors are primarily interested in how the product or service will be received in the market. Show them your research demonstrating and substantiating how the customer will benefit and be motivated to purchase so they will buy into your plan.

3. *Qualify the competition.* Qualify your product or service according to cost or time savings and revenue generation. Also show your projections for sales growth, how your product or service is superior to others, and how you intend to exploit the competitive advantage.

4. *Present your distribution plan.* Be specific as to how the company will sell and distribute its product or service. Clearly describe the

methods and what it will cost to get the product or service into the customers' hands.

5. *Exploit your company's uniqueness.* Explain what will give your company a competitive edge in the marketplace—special attributes like a patent, trade secrets, or copyrights. Explain in general your proprietary knowledge.

6. *Emphasize management strength.* Show proof that the company comprises highly qualified people who can cover all the bases. Indicate the incentives that will keep them together; and how they, the directors, and the advisers possess the necessary credibility. It's really helpful if you have worked together before.

7. *Present attractive projections.* Paint a realistic picture—substantiated by assumptions—of where your company will go with funding. Be detailed and keep it credible. Good, validated projections and forecasts are impressive.

8. *Zero in on possible funding sources.* Using the "different strokes for different folks" approach, design versions of the plan to fit the idiosyncrasies of each source you plan to approach. A banker's interest lies in stability, security, cash-flow coverage, and sound returns. A venture capitalist is interested in high leverage resulting in outrageous returns. Both want to know how the proceeds are going to be spent.

9. *Close with a bang.* Drive home the point that you're offering a good deal. Be explicit about how the investors will get their money back and when. Specify the return rates; state how the risk investor will receive a 30 percent or 50 percent compound annual return, or whatever you're offering. For lenders, show that their funds are adequately secured and that your cash flow more than covers their interest and principal payments.

Financing Choices

Although many Leading Edge start-ups are self-financed, most growth oriented entrepreneurial companies are constantly on the search for new capital—either through debt or equity—and it is seldom easy to come by. The savvy entrepreneur understands that raising money is a way of life. During the '90s, we've seen an evolution, not revolution, in financing. Strategic partnering, joint ventures, and subtle forms of private equity sharing are becoming the buzz words for the millennium.

Financing companies is done in stages and entrepreneurs must be flexible in identifying the latest trends in financing. Many first-timers erroneously believe that they can successfully generate sufficient cash flow on a near-term basis, then bootstrap their way to financial success.

This doesn't work, especially in many of today's medium- and high-tech companies.

Choices of Financing: Debt or Equity

Contrary to the dreams of many startup entrepreneurs, initial financing can be the hardest part of launching their new businesses. There are many popular misconceptions that an idea, a start-up team, and a preliminary business plan will get them in the venture capitalist door. They expect to exit, happily, with check in hand. They don't realize that traditional venture capital—funds that are supported by institutional investors—only finance a fraction of 1 percent of the new companies started each year. More than 90 percent of start-up money comes from private sources.

As you put together a business plan to use as a fundraising tool, the planning process itself, especially the financials section, will help you determine the type of financing you need and are able to accommodate.

After the plan, the second process is the actual raising of the financing, or *financial marketing*. Each way of raising money requires a different approach to the business plan. There are a number of sources of financing and a variety of forms of capital. Some are used to finance seed or start-up companies while others are used for expansion or high growth. Start-ups are usually limited to personal savings used as equity or personally secured subordinated debt. On the other hand, companies with a proven track record have a much larger choice of financing alternatives such as banks, venture capital firms, or public offerings. What all entrepreneurs soon discover is that there are several factors that they must constantly reckon with in pursuit of the elusive dollar. These are the dilution of equity ownership, potential restrictions on daily operating flexibility, and debt-imposed constraints on future growth.

For all intents and purposes, the entrepreneur has two basic choices when considering financing—debt or equity. This means pledging a part of one's life savings or giving away a piece of the business. Debt requires interest payments for a defined period of time. Equity pays profits or incurs losses. Commonly, you use both types of financing.

In simple terms, *debt* is borrowed money secured in some fashion using some type of asset for collateral. *Equity* is contributed capital, usually hard dollars, and is a purchase of part of your company. Debt may be secured by a personal signature only, and equity can also be in the form of a contributed asset.

But most often, new businesses require long-term debt or permanent equity capital to support major expansion and anticipated growth. The advantage of borrowing is that it is a relatively simple process to arrange.

It does not take a great deal of time and does not dilute equity ownership. The disadvantages are that it is a high-risk strategy as far as company growth is concerned, in that incurring debt subjects the company to a firm obligation, usually including the principals as cosigners. A downturn in business, or an increase in interest rates, could result in your inability to service (pay) debt payments.

Two Basic Sources of Financing

Just as there are two choices in financing, there are two basic sources of financing—self-funding and external funding. Self-funding, although the most preferable, is seldom the most practical.

Advantages of Self-Funding

Self-funding involves entrepreneurs investing their personal money. It has the following advantages:

- It allows the entrepreneurial team to take their time on their business plan and initial product development.
- It means the only financing source they have to answer to is themselves.
- It saves them the time otherwise devoted to finding financial partners.
- It establishes a strong internal discipline regarding the spending of funds.
- It frequently shortens the time needed to get the product/service to development stage.
- It usually lessens overhead costs.

The biggest point in favor of self-funding is the fact that it is the best way to build additional value, or *sweat equity,* into the company. A company with a prototype product or service that has been self-financed is worth much more than one, or several, individuals with just an idea.

External Funding Is More Complicated

External funding, while not as preferable in concept or seed stage, comes from a lot of different sources of both debt and equity, including informal and formal investors. The informal investors are family and friends. The formal include venture capital firms and the more formal type of investment groups usually brought together in a private placement. With all these possibilities, it makes external funding more complex.

There are pros and cons to all of these areas—debt, equity, self-funding, and external funding.

Top Entrepreneurs Use Combinations

Unlike oil and water, debt, equity, self-funding, and external funding do mix well. In fact, it's an entrepreneurial secret. Leading Edge companies must mix their financing sources and choices. Which to use, and when, becomes a matter of individual option although there are some pretty well established precedents.

Founders' personal investments, including both personal assets and family and friends' equity and loans, are usually what finances concept or seed stage companies. Development stage companies commonly seek funding from private placements, early-stage venture capital firms, and various grants from both foundations and government sources. Early-stage production companies may receive financing from bank loans, leasing companies, and research and development partnerships (for incremental product development). Strategic partnerships often are entered into at this stage with potential customers, suppliers, and manufacturers.

Companies at the next stage of ramping up, which is full-scale production and expanded marketing, often receive additional dollar injections. These come from second and larger rounds of traditional venture capital, larger companies that are looking for product distribution opportunities, institutional investors, more venture leasing companies (for manufacturing equipment), and additional strategic partners (often seeking secondary domestic and foreign manufacturing and distribution rights).

After the second stage, the entrepreneuring company has some heavy choices to consider. Here is where the harvest point is a natural. They still need more money (what's new?), but their choices are a lot broader: more venture capital, bridge or mezzanine financing while going public, being acquired (perhaps by one of the earlier-stage strategic partners), or selling out to a cash-rich company.

Do You Choose Debt or Equity?

If entrepreneurs use combinations of financing, how do we determine which and when? The use of debt almost always requires that some equity has come in first. A rough rule of thumb is that a dollar of early stage equity can support a dollar of debt—if there is some additional security to further back the debt. Lenders feel that a start-up has little ability to generate sales or profits. Consequently, the lender wants to have its debt secured, and even then, may feel that the asset value will be decreasing with time and there's always the possibility that management may not be up to the company-building challenge.

Debt will most likely be short-term (one year or less), to be paid back from sales. *Short-term debt* is traditionally used for working capital and small equipment purchases. *Long-term borrowing* (one to five years) can be used for some working capital needs, but usually is assigned to finance property or equipment that serves as collateral for the debt. Although commercial banks are the most common source of short-term debt, there are more choices for long-term financing. Equipment manufacturers provide some, as does the Small Business Administration (SBA), various state agencies, and leasing companies.

While it's true that entrepreneurs can finance start-ups with more debt than equity, there are some distinct disadvantages. If they negotiate extended credit terms with several suppliers, this restricts their flexibility to negotiate prices. Heavily leveraged (i.e., debt-financed) companies are constantly undercapitalized and experience continuing cash flow problems as they grow. Monitoring a strained cash flow requires that a lot of management time be diverted from company operations. It also negatively affects the balance sheet, making it difficult to obtain additional equity or debt.

On the other hand, there are two big positives in using debt. Debt doesn't decrease or dilute the entrepreneur's equity position and it provides nice returns on invested capital. Second, interest payments on debt are tax deductible. However, if credit costs go up or sales don't meet projections, cash flows really get pinched and bankruptcy can ensue.

Leading Edge entrepreneurial companies use varying combinations of debt and equity. They determine which is the most advantageous for the particular stage of growth they're financing. Their aim is to create increasingly higher valuations for the company to enhance future financing.

8
Setting Up Your Leading Edge Plan

Writing the business plan can be an exciting time for the entrepreneur. As you research, make assumptions and draw up details, the company becomes a living entity. You are the first to see how it looks, where it goes, and why it makes a profit.

As the foundation to your company, your business plan and all of its parts must fit and work well together, with no unaddressed cracks, flaws, or gaps. As your business unfolds on paper, it becomes personal and, if you are thorough, you learn how to deal with the inevitable problems that are bound to occur.

Because no two companies are alike, the content of business plans varies significantly. Although the main headings cover similar topics, the format of each section—its headings, text, and graphics—must provide two pictures: the overview with a road map, plus proof of its ability to make a profit that surpasses its investment.

The real point is that in a Leading Edge business plan, these two pictures are one and the same. The picture up front must match the numbers in back. Both must be complete, make sense, and belong to one another. If you are honest and thorough you will know when they meld.

Take advantage of the opportunity to run your company on paper as you write your business plan. Become familiar with its parts and concepts *before* investing. The plan prepares you to deal with likely business problems, including the unexpected and unplanned. A good job of developing a Leading Edge plan will show you why planned small companies make more than twice the money of their unplanned competitors. Most important of all, a good business plan will give you confidence about knowing what to do when you open your company's doors.

The Leading Edge Outline

Every plan should include some specific information, whether you write it for yourself or others. A Leading Edge plan encompasses several sections. The actual text and locations will vary widely, but your plan should have sections that include:

- An executive summary
- The business
- Products and services
- Industry and market
- Marketing strategy
- Operations
- Management
- A financial analysis
- Supporting documents

The following chapters detail how to create a Leading Edge plan that helps you obtain funding or successfully plan the operations of your company on paper. Although the information may, at times, seem general in nature, many of the suggestions which initially seem obvious often get missed or overlooked when writing the plan. It is up to you add lots of detail, meticulously gathered and presented in succinct Leading Edge form.

How Your Plan Makes an Impact

We have received plans leather bound, as videos, on computer disk, and through our modems. It's not the package, it is the content that is important. The challenge is to present your plan clearly, simply, factually, and without a lot of narrative. Make an impact based on content; how the underlying facts, assumptions, text, graphics, calculations, and estimates clearly demonstrate each point; and how well all of them fit together.

Formatting Your Plan

Left justified type is preferable to fully justified (where both sides of the text on the page are even). Fully justified is difficult to read and your intention is to get the reader to read your whole document, not skip parts of it because the report is hard to read. Use bold, underlining, and italics when appropriate, but don't overdo it. NEVER type your narrative in all caps, it is very difficult to read. Make sure your print is dark and clear.

Leading Edge Format Points
· · · · ·

- Neatly formatted word processing (what we used to call type-written)

- Typed or desk-top-published with clear, dark print

- 8½″ × 11″ white paper (color is okay for dividers)

- Charts and graphics when useful

- Double-spaced lines

- Length of 40 to 50 pages is usually sufficient

- Spiral plastic bound

- Applicable diagrams, drawings, photos, or product brochures

- Additional exhibits referred to and available

Believe it or not, the amount of white space on your plan's pages makes a comment about your understanding and organization of its concepts. Use bullets to present multiple, related points. Vary sentence length and paragraph styles to give the reader's eyes a rest. Write and print on one side of the page only, so the reader can make notes on the facing page.

Use one inch margins all around for the reader's use in making comments or noting questions. (Yes, this means that if you expect to get the copy back, it may not be useful for passing out to someone else. On the other hand, it gives you the opportunity to review what the reader was thinking if they made margin notes as they reviewed your plan.)

Adding Graphs, Pictures, Drawings, Charts, and Tables

Today's world is filled with sound bites, spins, and MTV. Practically every television commercial has multiple quick cuts. Everyone is too busy, too sophisticated, and too bombarded with multiple images and overexposed to glitz. If, when your plan is thumbed through, the appearance is page after page of single-spaced lines, it won't get read. You have to look for every opportunity to break up your text with a graphic, even if it's a simple point chart. We're a highly visual society and this also applies to creating a Leading Edge business plan.

One great place to use a picture of your operation or of your product is the first page inside the front cover. Especially if its color—economical today with color copiers—it sets the tone for an easy-to-read plan.

Forty Pages Is Enough

Your plan doesn't have to be 40 pages if you can say everything in 20. But it does mean that for most companies 80 pages is way too much. Aim for 40 and if you end up with 50—after some super editing—that's okay. However, we've never seen a plan that held our interest long after 40 pages.

It's very common that you also have one or several support documents. These may be your detailed marketing plan or detailed financial back-up. You may need product support in the form of testimonial letters or technical papers and documents on test results and marketing studies. Keep those separate from the content in your 40 page plan, referring to the support documents as needed.

Binding Your Plan

Get the finished plan bound. Three ring binders are fine; folders with a plastic stick on the edge are not. The binding stick falls off all the time and gets lost in file drawers, on desks, and in brief cases. For the reader to give your plan the attention it deserves, it must lay flat when it is open. Spiral binding is best; just be sure you leave some extra space in the left-hand margin for the binding.

The Cover Sheet

Here's your first chance to shine—don't lose it. All of the information shown in the box on the following page *must* be on the cover page.

Include spaces for a plan number and the name of the person reading the plan. Plans with the reader's name on the cover are okay, but don't score any big points. Many attorneys insist that the company keeps track of how many and to whom plans are submitted. This is an individual decision but not a bad idea. (Keep a log with the copy number, name of the reader, reader's phone number, and the date you issued the plan.)

A second cover sheet item is the use of a disclaimer. Your attorney will naturally encourage it. It seldom offends readers and it does provide the company with a sort of insurance policy as well as prevent casual readers from "pirating" your information. And you thought that disclaimers were just to prevent people from stealing your ideas. A good general disclaimer is shown on the following page.

A Leading Edge Point: The Cover Sheet
• • • • •

Indicate full formal name of company
ABC Company/ABC Corporation/ABC Inc.
(If you have a logo, use it.)

Indicate ownership status
A sole proprietorship/A New York corporation

List full street address
555 West Fifth, Suite 55, Anytown, State, ZIP USA

List mailing address if different
Mail address = P.O. Box 55, Anytown, State, ZIP USA

List phone and FAX Number
List Company Web site address (URL)

List principal contact name and title
Mr. E. E. Entrepreneur,—President
List e-mail address
(Home phone number optional)

(Disclaimer text)
Date the Plan—Month and year
Plan Number_____

A Leading Edge Point: The General Disclaimer
• • • • •

Your cover sheet should contain a disclaimer like the one below:

"This Business Plan has been prepared by the management team of insert your company's name, and is being furnished to select individuals for the sole purpose of attracting potential financing to the Company. This Business Plan is a confidential document that contains ideas, concepts, methods, and other proprietary information. Readers are to treat the information contained herein as confidential and may not copy any of these materials without the written permission of the Company."

The disclaimer can be set in smaller, unobtrusive type at the bottom of the cover page.

Table of Contents

A Table of Contents gives the reader an overview of what to expect. It also acts as a guide for specific topic identification and for quick reading or review. In addition, it saves time when searching for specific information. A well defined table of contents forces the business plan writer to logically structure the sequence of the presentation.

Tables of Contents should be well-designed with categorized section names and page numbers. There are several schools of thought as to sequential page numbering versus section or chapter numbering. It doesn't make a lot of difference, just be sure you stay consistent.

Start with the Executive Summary. Page numbers run through the last page of text. If you use section or chapter numbering, each major section is given a sequential number and the pages that follow are numbered accordingly. As an example, the section on The Product might be 3-1 through 3-12, and the section on Management could start with 8-1 through 8-6.

Frequently you will have subsections within a section. These subsections or headings should be listed in the table of contents. For instance, the Product would have subsections on: description, industry, competition, advantages/disadvantages.

The same goes for charts, tables, diagrams and graphs. Each of these should have a separate listing in your table of contents. Yes, this means that your Table of Contents can easily get to be two pages in length. However, it doesn't hurt to make it single spaced. Also, remember to include the items in your Appendix.

The Executive Summary

This may be the most important part of your plan. It describes the company, the product, and the market opportunity in very concise words that also entice the reader to continue. It should be to the point. Be cautioned to avoid repeating anything; it can spoil your efforts.

The Executive Summary is the first thing read by your potential investors and they may not read further if you have not captured their interest. The summary briefly sets forth the major elements of the plan and its contents, taking key sentences from each section of the plan to overview the project for the reader. Consider using your mission statement or a brief visionary type of paragraph; keep it to two or three pages.

The Executive Summary is also the place to note that you have additional back-up information in the form of a marketing plan, research data, detailed financials, testimonials, scientific papers, magazine or newspaper articles, or other support documents.

The best way to write an attention-grabbing Executive Summary is to take a stab at it when you first start to write your plan. This helps you organize your initial thoughts as to the key points of your plan. However, we suggest that you revise it as you go along. You'll find that as you do more research, discover new areas of and about your business, that you'll need to add new parts to your Executive Summary, as well as eliminate others. This continuing process helps you further refine your thinking.

Finally, when your plan is finished, write a brand new Executive Summary taking key parts and sentences from all your finished sections. Compare this new summary to your last revision and also against your very first draft. Then combine the best of all three. This projects your original thoughts and emotions, developing thoughts, and final thoughts, into an attention-grabbing document.

Setting Up

We have shown you an overview of the need to make an impact with your plan, how to size and format it, and the use of graphics to grab the reader's attention. Your Executive Summary is just that, a two to three page overview, whose purpose is to define and briefly outline the company, its opportunity, its mission in business, its products and services, and its goals or expected financial returns. The scene is now set to delve into the details, hard facts, and the process of writing a Leading Edge business plan.

9 ·

The Business Description

The Business Description is the first section of your plan after the Executive Summary. In two or three pages you should briefly describe why the company exists, its structure, where it has been, where it is going, who owns it, and what makes it special.

This section of your business plan covers several items, each of which can either be its own section, or combined with other sections. The purpose of these items is to give the reader a capsule overview of:

- The type of business (wholesale, retail, manufacturing, service)
- The company's mission and its goals
- The company's contact address and facilities
- The company's structure or organization—its form of ownership
- The company's history, including notable accomplishments and setbacks (if applicable)
- The company's products or services
- What makes the company special (from competition)
- The current status of its industry, and where the company fits in

It is easy to describe your business if you are going to buy, operate, or expand a hardware store, candy shop, or a used car lot. Although each takes a lot of entrepreneurial skill to operate, everyone is familiar with these types of businesses.

However, if you're starting a unique service business, or turning a technology innovation into a company, the task of describing your business is more difficult. Your goal for now is a short, clear, concise, and simple set of statements. Details and subtle nuances will come as you progress through the plan. Right now, the reader needs a firm understanding of just what business you are in.

The Business Narrative

In one or two paragraphs briefly describe whether your company is a wholesale, retail, manufacturing, service, distribution, or other type of firm. Give an example of its main product or service, and the cities, states, or countries where it intends to sell its products or services.

Consider addressing many of the following points:

- When do you plan to start or open? Is timing important? Are there cyclical peaks and valleys in your selling periods? What hours and days are you open? Why?
- Does your industry have a special nature which affects your business? Is the business seasonal in nature? Does it sell or distribute products or services in a particular or unusual manner?
- Does location matter? What about information, experience, technology, or access?

If you are a principal or sole owner, you should write a short paragraph that tells what direct management experience you have, or that exists on the management team. Will consultants or advisers be helping you?

The Purpose of Your Company

This section briefly defines what business the company is engaged in. Many an entrepreneur, even after starting a company, may not know what business he or she is in. A mission statement, or statement of purpose, tells the plan's readers, that the entrepreneur knows:

- Who is the customer for the company's products and services.
- Which products or services the company sells, to whom, where, and at what level (retail, wholesale, distributor, online).
- Why its markets, locations, level of business volume, or other aspects of this business approach were chosen.

These critical concepts can be presented in a few paragraphs. A mission statement helps you focus your awareness of where your company is, where it is going, why it is on a particular course, and when—if ever—the company will depart from this course. Your mission statement can also answer:

- Why will you succeed?
- Why are you going to be profitable?

Goals

Briefly present your company's operational goals.

- Where do you wish the company to be in one year? After two or three? What volume of sales will it have?
- What type of changes will it undergo in the form of management, personnel, resources, facilities, products, services, markets, or sales methods?
- Will you sell the company at some point, form a strategic alliance or partnership, merge with another firm, license your technology, sell stock, or attempt to operate a lifestyle enterprise for the foreseeable future?

The Company's Address

List the company's main address, including its full name, street address, postal box number, telephone numbers, e-mail, city, state, country, zip code, and the name and position (if you have one) of the person to contact for more information.

Leading Edge Online/Virtual Facilities Description
●●●●●

Two recent, explosive trends have changed the nature of where and how companies operate:

1. A growing number of large and small companies operate online, either over the Internet, or with an intranet, or extranet, using the World Wide Web or other telecommunications protocols for marketing, sales, distribution, customer relations, business alliances, or other reasons.

2. A growing number of companies operate from "virtual" locations. They will sell products or services that are created, designed, manufactured, stored, shipped, distributed, sold by other firms, while operating from a remote location.

If your company plans to run using any of these factors, the Address and Facilities section is a good place to present why you made this choice, plus a brief description—in one or two sentences—of which choices you made. The details will go into Product, Marketing, or other sections.

For a small company this section can include any other locations, facilities, and resources the company uses to conduct business. The locations may include a brief description of their features or qualities, such as their size, location, or special nature that makes them meaningful to the company.

Company Structure or Organization

What is the legal structure of your company? Provide the date and city where the company was founded. If you're incorporated, give the state of incorporation. If you started out as a sole-proprietorship, then formed a partnership and then incorporated, state the dates of progression. If you started as an "S " Corporation and now intend to change to a "C " Corporation, then so state. Some items to consider when writing this section, include:

- Is the company a sole proprietorship? A partnership? A general/limited partnership? An "S" corporation? A "C" corporation? An LLC (Limited Liability Company)? PC (Professional Corporation)?
- Does the company intend, at some time, to raise investment capital? Does its form of ownership reflect this intention? When are you planning to start this funding?
- If the company is, or intends to become, a stock company, what type of stock, warrants, or options will it authorize and distribute? Will the company follow the traditional path with a market maker, or will it attempt a DPO (direct public offering) over the Internet or through a SCOR (Small Company Offering).
- Will the form of the ownership change during the life of the business plan?

Every form of ownership has virtues and drawbacks. In the past, when most companies had equity or debt financing, the type of ownership had to fit the needs of the investors or creditors. That's still true. For self-funded companies, the correct form of ownership can help protect the entrepreneur's initial investment. Planning the form of ownership helps the entrepreneur visualize situations—both positive and negative—where outside capital comes into the company, and what to do in those cases.

Founding Principals

Provide the names of the original founders, shareholders, and directors, if any. Make note of the recent (over the past five years) changes. Show how much ownership, in what form, and how much each person owns. Are there special ownership arrangements to be granted in the future, such as a performance-based stock or equity transfer?

The History of the Company

The company history tells the story of how the company originated and how it has grown. It explains who founded the company, what business problem was solved by its formation, plus any significant achievements, milestones, or setbacks along the way.

Are you starting a new company? Are you buying an existing business? Is this an expansion of your existing operations? Are you spinning off a division of a larger company? This should be just a simple, straight forward commentary.

Significant Changes

If there have been some significant changes in the structure, management, or ownership of the company, discuss the predecessors and these changes in a brief and factual manner.

Achievements, Disappointments, Advances, and Setbacks

Other than brand new enterprises, most businesses have had some prior experiences, both good and bad. It helps the reader if you discuss these. However, do so very briefly and with a positive bent.

Maybe you received a big order and then couldn't get the financing to fill it. Perhaps one of the principals was forced to drop out for personal reasons and this set you back six months while you found a replacement. Then again, a new technology may have appeared and you had to go back to the drawing boards to redesign for your product. Or you may have had a bad *beta test*. (A beta test is a second generation test of a company's product. It is usually conducted at a prospective customer's site or in operations where the product is tested in a "real-world" environment.)

You're lucky if you had a setback that resulted in your making a major breakthrough. Emphasize how the learning experience has made your product or service even better, or that the breakthrough will catapult the company into a position of industry leadership. Regardless of the story, indicate how you and your management team overcame the odds and have now persevered to become even more successful.

Proprietary Industry Relationships

This is where you can describe your industry and how the company fits into it. In one or two sentences explain how the industry presents or sells products or services. Will your company affiliate, form alliances, or rely on other firms for any of its major functions? Does your company have a unique competitive niche, a proprietary technology innovation, or some other factor that gives it an advantage over how the industry normally does business? If so, this is a good place to briefly describe it.

A Few Points to Consider

As you write this section, think about these points:

- Have you talked with prospective customers?
- Have you talked with competitors?
- Have you set up suppliers?
- What credit terms are you going to make?
- Is yours a quantity or quality business?
- Is it a mature product/service? Has it been on the market for a long time? How long is your product's life cycle?
- If you sell capital goods used by businesses versus consumer goods:
  - How many inventory turns do you expect?
  - What is the shelf life of your product?
  - How critical is your proximity to principal suppliers? Customers?

A Final Point

An underlying theme for the Leading Edge business plan writer to remember is to keep your narrative simple and direct. Think about this every time you put pen to paper. The simpler you write, the better you'll catch the reader's attention. This leaves them the opportunity to grasp the meat of your project without having to stop and try to figure out what you're saying.

Remember: the goal in the Business Section is to give one, brief thumbnail sketch of the total company. The details come in the following sections.

10 Products or Services

After you describe the general business of your company, your next challenge becomes to plainly describe your company's product or service. To succeed with your company, you must know your product or service. To succeed in obtaining capital, you have to be able to clearly describe your product or service. It should be as short, direct, and as easy to read as you can write it. Make the major points with a minimum of rhetoric.

Unless your plan is going only to those persons who are specialists in your business or industry, assume you are writing for the layperson. This even applies to venture capitalists. They are generalists and often don't possess the detailed knowledge of industry-specific jargon. Use words and phrases that nonspecialists can understand. If you tend to write technical descriptions, then it's very much worth the time and money to engage a professional writer. All technological or scientific types of companies *must* put a glossary in their business plans. Nothing is more frustrating to the lay business plan reader then to try to absorb a lot of technical jargon. The hardest part is to try to remember the meaning of a particular phrase or acronym when it was explained five paragraphs or ten pages ago. A Glossary helps because the reader can easily turn to the Glossary when confronting this problem.

Overall Points

Address the following points as applicable, keeping in mind that you're after a simple, straightforward description:

- What is the product? (describe physical characteristics; size, weight, color, packaging)
- What is the service? (define nature)

- What does it do? (for products)
- What service do you deliver?
- What is the primary application? Secondary applications?
- What need does it fill?
- Who are the customers?
- Who makes the buying decision? (if buyer and user are different, what's the relationship between them?)
- How does the customer benefit from it?
- What makes it different from its competition?
- Emphasize its distinctive features.
- State advantages and disadvantages.
- State strengths and weaknesses.
- How complex or simple is it (from the user standpoint)?
- What are the results of using it?
- Why will the customer buy it?
- What type of regulations—product liability, environmental, zoning—are relevant (both in selling and in using)?
- What type of training is needed, to sell or use it?
- What proprietary positions do you have? (patents, trademarks, copyrights, trade secrets, processes)
- Discuss head-starts over competition (which establish favorable or entrenched positions).
- How does your existing product or service relate to companion or multiple product/service lines?
- Does your product's use require disposables? (the old "sell razors at cost and make profits from replacement blades" story)
- What stage of development is the company in? (this can apply to service as well as products)
  - Concept—formulation or testing?
  - Design—general or detailed?
  - Prototype—stage one or many models?
  - Production—sample or limited numbers?
  - Marketing—testing or advanced?
  - Production—limited or full?
  - What is the price sensitivity? If your product or service is commodity-driven, are you in the low end or high end price range?
  - Can you build up your perceived value?

Determine Your Unique Selling Point (USP)

Describe your *Unique Selling Point*. Every successful business has one. If you cannot find yours, you had better find one, find someone who can, or get out of business. Sometimes it's very simple; like:

- a product that is patented;
- the unique personality of the president, who also does the sales;
- a significantly lower selling price; or
- user time is drastically saved.

Other times, it's very complex. As an example: IBM, as a manufacturer of large computers, is not known by its users for technical superiority or low prices. Their USP is customer service.

Give this area careful thought. Uncovering your USP is a Leading Edge business plan point and it needs definition early on in your plan, right up in your Executive Summary.

What's Your Product Life Cycle?

Both products and services have *life cycles,* or a defined period for how long the product or service has a sales value in the marketplace. Most products/services follow a cycle where the revenue is small at the time it's introduced into the market. Then the revenues continue to grow over time through the *growth* phase into what is called the *mature* phase, and then decline until negligible sales revenues are received.

It's important that you determine what the time span of these cycles are. Most industries have pretty well defined *life cycle* time periods. You can get a feel for these by contacting the trade associations that follow your particular industry. Better yet, what is the *collective feel* from the members of your management team who are most likely industry experienced? Investors in your project want to know that you have a grasp of these facts as life cycles also effect the research and development of your new product/service. Some industry life cycles keep getting shorter and shorter—especially high-technology driven companies.

One Product Won't Do

If you are the inventor or have discovered a single product, it is very difficult to self-finance the product to a large market. We recommend that you sell or lease the rights to it to an existing company that manufactures or markets a similar product. The world markets are just too big and move too fast to take a chance that you can produce a single product and gain and hold a sales leader position in a timely manner.

If on the other hand, your product has multiple applications or markets, plus the capability to spin-off new versions in additional models or sizes, or it can be presented or sold quickly online, explore the possibilities with some very knowledgeable and trusted industry-savvy people. They may be able to network you into some advantageous partnering opportunities.

A Leading Edge Example
• • • • •

Construction Delivery Corporation (CDC)

The Construction Delivery Corporation created a proprietary software product called "Delivery," that makes it possible to download and view blueprints over a secure, password-protected, Internet site. This software makes it faster and easier to find and bid on different projects—from anywhere in the world. This opens construction projects in all fields to a host of new bidders.

What are the software's Unique Selling Points?

- Its product innovation allows just-in-time delivery convenience, on a 24-7 basis, at a much lower cost than its competitors.

- It's virtual, online presence costs less to use and makes it possible for companies to place many more project bids, at a lower cost, than ever before.

How does CDC protect itself from being a one-product company?

- It offers a subscription service at multiple levels to contractors.

- It goes out to all building trades, across industry and national boundaries.

- It develops improvements and additional features to stay ahead of the competition.

- It leverages its technology by forming an alliance with selected industry leaders.

These strategies, and others, makes it possible for CDC to compete against larger, more experienced, firms.

Leading Edge Growth

Leading Edge growth is what gets venture capitalists very excited. If they see a company that is into a market that offers the opportunity for the company to grow at a very fast rate, they'll be much more interested in investing. High growth, although difficult to quantify in dollars, percentages, or people, can be thought of as 100 percent-per-annum, compounded, over a five year period. But be cautioned—these are entry level rates and you had better be able to firmly substantiate your projections.

What's Your Address?

The subject of the importance of location, location, location for a retail operation comes up later in this chapter. However, your physical address may be important for any type of company. If you're in the mail order business in your local community, some people won't buy if they perceive you're physically located in what is considered a bad side of town. So, get a post office box or private mail service site on a "classy" street. And get a Web site.

If your company is aligned with a particular industry, you may be required to relocate in its known area; e.g., Silicon Valley, Route 128, Research Triangle. In larger cities, it may be to your advantage to relocate to a specific part of town; e.g., downtown, an industrial park, a business incubator.

If clients will visit your offices, the physical features of your building may be important; e.g., plush high rise offices, peaceful office park, shared secretarial services. We're also talking about what floor you're on, air conditioning, close-in or ample reserved parking, proximity to warehouse space, and the list goes on with particular items important to your specific business or industry.

The point is that if location is important in the eyes of the investor, or if you have an ideal facility, this is the place in your plan to discuss these factors. They may be key points to the description of your business.

Products . . . Services . . . Retailing: Adding Value

Different industries require specific approaches when writing a business plan. A successful Leading Edge business plan (1) shows you recognize the industry-specific approaches by addressing them, and (2) shows how you add value to your manufacturing, service, or retailing project.

Value is created by finding new ways to solve the inherent contradiction of economic life—trying to get more for less. A company's success, measured by return on shareholders equity, is derived from its ability to create value for its customers. Value derives from the cost savings or capability enhancements made possible for the customer. Point out in your plan how you do, or intend to, add value for your customers and to your business.

Adding Value When Manufacturing a Product

The first major point of discussion in every manufacturing-oriented business is whether to have the work done in-house or to subcontract it out. You need to address the advantages/disadvantages of each and justify why you chose which method. Manufacturing companies are usually *capital intensive.* They have a lot of up-front investment in machinery and inventory (both raw goods and finished inventory), and consequently are at the high end of the investment risk spectrum. Whether you are manufacturing in-house or subcontracting, you must address the following manufacturing points:

- Do you manufacture on a continuous (long run) or intermittent (short run) basis? Long runs mean equipment and personnel produce the same item for extended time periods. Short runs mean production is stopped frequently or at predetermined times to produce a variety of products (often customized).
- Production down-time is expensive. How do you justify the costs?
- How are you positioned to take advantage of the constant technology changes in manufacturing? There are a lot of changes from raw material improvements to robotics. How do you adapt to these on a continuing basis?
- Foreign manufacturers always seem to be able to produce new products or develop knock-offs quickly. How do you confront this problem?
- Inventory control is extremely important. How will you minimize excess inventory? Explain how you will control/track inventory.
- Quality control is very important for manufacturing. Explain your company's approach to this increasingly important area.
- List the barriers of entry for new competitors. Cite the capital-intensive nature of manufacturing, patent protection, special expertise, large capital outlays, intricate processes, proprietary knowledge, etc.
- Cite management expertise in production. Show that you not only understand the product, but that you also understand how to manufacture it.

Do you have a *Production Manual?* Every manufacturer should have one that indicates items such as lead time for purchasing raw materials, second sources for all items, maximum inventory levels (both raw and finished goods), and labor and equipment requirements. Let the plan reader know that this manual is available as a separate business plan exhibit.

In-house manufacturing. If you are manufacturing in-house, be sure you address the following points:

- *Cost justification of expensive machinery.* You have to be sure each part you produce with expensive machinery is a high value-added part to justify manufacturing it in-house versus subcontracting.

- *Stability and justification of labor.* Labor is quite often the most expensive part of manufacturing. Consequently, you need to justify both full- and part-time labor sources—that you can keep them employed without having slack periods. Keep training simple. Be sure you can regain volume after a production slowdown. Cover union/nonunion issues.
- *Can you subcontract some of your manufacturing capabilities?* In other words, can you act as a subcontractor to others because you have a specialized piece of machinery or excess capacity?

Subcontract manufacturing. If you have chosen to subcontract your manufacturing, be sure you consider addressing the following points:

- Subcontracting can reduce basic overhead costs in labor, space, machinery and inventory investment, maintenance, and management headaches. If this is true in your case, point out specifics.
- Who is doing the production design and production planning? Subcontract manufacturing requires a clear understanding of who is going to pay for these areas as well as the setup or retooling costs and amortization of tooling or dies.
- Will your company have to advance monies for the purchase of raw materials and if so, how do you control this inventory and any waste?
- Cite alternate suppliers, especially for critical parts or materials.

Adding Value When You're Providing a Service

Service businesses are a growing, very diverse part of our economy. They range from accountants to zookeepers. They include medical care, carpentry, house cleaning, parking lot maintenance, delivery services of all types, personal shopping services, technical writing/editing, computing , and the list goes on. Some are aimed at personal services, others strictly for the business market. However, they all have some common areas to be addressed in a Leading Edge business plan.

In a service business, where your product is intangible, the results are judged subjectively. The opinion about the quality of your service is made by the service receiver. The person performing determines the level of quality of the service provided. If you're a sole proprietor, you determine quality on the spot. If you employ others, you need to emphasize to them how important quality of service is. Quality is never an accident; it is always the result of high intention, sincere effort, intelligent direction, continuing training and skillful execution. It is a Leading Edge business secret.

Time. Service providers sell their time, which is perishable. They sell their expertise—also perishable. You must show the business plan reader that you recognize the value of time, that you know how to efficiently schedule it, and show that you know how to effectively update expertise. Expertise updating comes in the form of attending industry-specific seminars, participating in trade shows, taking special classes, bringing in trainers, and generally keeping up with new industry trends.

Industry barriers. The good news is that a lot of service businesses are easy to get into. They may not require a large dollar commitment to get started—for some, you may only need a phone number. Others may require an office, a store front, or an elaborate Web site. The bad news is that it's easy for someone to start a competing business. Analyze your industry and see if you can determine an effective way to deter competitors from copying your service. It's a tough assignment, but you might find a protected niche.

Quality depends on you. We hear the phrase, "We care," every day. We're bombarded by advertising, in all media, from all types of businesses, about one company or another giving the best service. It's a new trend after years of companies providing poor service to customers. Loyalty to a service provider has often been replaced by a discount coupon in the newspaper. There is a limit to how much you can cut prices and still stay in business. The result is that you must provide quality customer service to stay even, and absolutely superior service to get ahead.

Keep in touch. It costs service companies dearly to gain new customers. Once you have them, be sure you keep them. Do this by staying in touch.

Be sure your communications are interactive. A reminder of how good you are is just another ad. If it includes a discount coupon or special offer, it gives clients a reason to return. Stress the fact that you appreciate your customers. Develop a distinctive image—one that sets you apart from competition. And always approach your business with creativity. If you posture your service properly and uniquely, it can be shown how Leading Edge service-based investments can pay large dollar returns. The examples of how are numerous, and you should use your imagination to supplement this list:

- Web sites
- Newsletters
- Flyers
- Mailers

- Discount coupons
- Preferred customer rates
- Telemarketing reminders
- Referral bonuses
- And an overlooked favorite—the customer satisfaction survey

Service Adds Up

Although service businesses are usually thought of as smaller companies that can provide a very comfortable living to the owners, many can be extremely profitable. The secret of course is high markups. Your Leading Edge business plan challenge is to show potential investors how you will make both them and you a lot of bucks.

Adding Value in Your Retailing Business

The retail industry continues to make some significant evolutions. We have gone from a domination by large department stores such as JC Penney's and Sears to warehouses or superstores. Today, these superstores are frequently surrounded by boutique stores.

Superstores. They offer a broad and deep merchandise selection in a physically large store, with both national and private brand products. They are short on fancy interiors and personal service. Instead, they promote low margins, low prices, and quantity savings. Big parking lots and self-service combine to offer value in convenient, one-stop shopping.

Boutiques. These shops, on the other hand, promote a specialized, narrow product segment, often aimed at filling emotional and lifestyle needs. They add value by offering unique—often handmade—products (usually with high markups), a high quality personalized service, and a unique atmosphere.

If you're a boutique retailer, you need to be very mindful of the increasing trend that today's customers are far more demanding than in the past. They also frequently view shopping as a recreational activity as much as a necessity—especially in a boutique or specialty store. You must stay on top of your customers' fast-changing tastes and cultivate shopping as an art. If you buy too much, you're stuck with markdowns, (unless that's your specialty), and if you buy too little, you lose sales revenues. Showing how you approach these points is your Leading Edge business plan challenge.

Off-site shopping. As our lives become busier, and our street traffic gets worse, a growing number of people are learning to go shopping on the World Wide Web for goods and services they used to buy in stores. The advent of interactive, automated, directed, colorful, multimedia information and materials, sold using secure electronic transactions, has led to an explosive growth in online markets.

Likewise, having fax, e-mail, or toll-free ordering (especially to supplement a print catalog or ads) will broaden your customer base.

In all off-site shopping, add value with specials, discounts, etc., so customers want to stay in touch with you.

Location . . . Location . . . Location. Prove, in no uncertain terms, that you have a superior location. This is another Leading Edge point, especially from an investor's perspective. You do this by assembling demographics that show insatiable buyer support for your retail concept. This must include site maps or studies that validate traffic counts.

Here's an opportunity to inject graphics into your plan. Use several maps that lead the investor into a detailed plot plan of your location. First a city map, then a neighborhood map, then your site. If you're in a shopping center, show your exact location inside the center, noting the major stores that draw traffic your way. Almost all communities have traffic counts on most main thoroughfares. Sometimes you have to go to your state highway department to get them. Regardless, if you depend on auto traffic, show the numbers (in graph form) and don't forget to justify how you'll get the traffic to stop in. If you depend on visitor traffic online, show how your name, keyword used in search, your publicity, or other promotions will bring traffic to your site.

Customers Buy Solutions

Retailing is a fickle, trendy, economically fluctuating type of business. It's a customer-driven business and your love of people and understanding of your market should come across undeniably in your business plan.

Above all, remember when writing this section on your business description, that *customers buy solutions, not devices.* Your challenge here is to convince the business plan reader that you have a solution that encompasses the device or service. In the example, the Leading Edge company, Construction Delivery Corporation, did not sell its technology; it sold a better way to do business. When you're describing your product or service, keep your descriptions solution oriented.

11 The Market

Entrepreneurs usually have the most problems with the market sections of their business plans. They either do not understand—or choose to ignore—how their companies will generate revenues in the real marketplace.

This chapter defines your market to a wider extent than the feasibility study chapter. The next chapter discuss strategies to approach the market and make sales.

There are three distinct areas of the market: your *industry*, *customers* and *competition*. You should profile each one. It is very important that these sections be founded on substantiated facts. Every number, statistic, and fact *must* be sourced; i.e., where did you get the facts? You can do this in the text, footnotes, or Appendix references. If you're citing voluminous reports or statistical information, note that you have the information available for further review as separate documents (see Chapter 16).

Nothing destroys your credibility quicker than bad statistics. Remember, the readers of your plan may know a lot about your business and they may have statistics of their own. Don't guess: be sure to explain assumptions, draw succinct conclusions, and include the latest information.

Prepare an Industry Profile

What is the size and nature of your industry? How old is it? Discuss pertinent industry trends—past, present, and future. Refer to trade association data if available. Don't be afraid to draw a simple conclusion as to the fact that the market is growing (or consolidating), at what rate, and for what reasons. Display historical and projected statistical data on total industry sales in both units and dollars. If applicable, break these out further for geographical areas: international, national, regional, or local.

Remember that your objective here is to outline the maximum potential of your industry. You are establishing the justification for your marketing and financial projections. Consider the following areas:

- What are the total sizes of your industry and intended specific market(s) by:
  - international
  - national
  - regional
  - local
- Look at the above from the perspective of your full product line, segments of your product line, and multiple markets and target markets. Detailed breakouts are invaluable.
- What are the historical, current, and projected growth rates?
- Are any social/economic/political changes affecting the market for your product or service?
- What are the changing needs in the actual use of your product or service?
- Have you conducted any formal marketing studies? Informal? Are any independent or industry studies available?
- Discuss any new product, service, or industry development.

Offer available statistical data on both sales in U.S. dollars and units sold. Use charts, graphs, and tables to make the presentation clearer (and more impressive).

Prepare a Customer Profile

Who's your market? This is where you describe:

- What persons or businesses form your market.
- Where they can be found.
- Why they purchase your product or service rather than another.
- Whether it appeals to a single individual or to groups.
- The buyer and the user, who may not always be the same person (Consider how direct advertising by the pharmaceutical companies now has patients asking doctors to prescribe specific medicines.)
- Any political influences.
- Briefly, market coverage—local, regional, national, or international.

Use the above points and the following questions to guide you in profiling your customers. Keep in mind that your goal is to provide as complete a definition of the persons or firms that will buy your product or service, as possible (See Chapter 4 on Research).

- Who are your customers? What's their economic makeup? Cite some demographics and use charts and tables if possible. What's their age mix, nationality, sex, marital status, religion, or political attitude, if pertinent? Does education, occupation, size of family, or lifestyle matter?
- How far away do they live or work? Is this important? Is density of population (urban, suburban, rural), size of city, or type of climate important?
- Are they Fortune 100 or 1000 corporations, small proprietorships, or individual consumers?
- How many of them are there (potential market)? How many do you need (market share)?
- Do they buy more than one item or service at a time?
- How do the following impact the buying decision?
  - Price
  - Quality
  - Warranty
  - Service
  - Color
  - Size
  - Weight
  - Discounts
  - Payment terms
- Where do they make purchases?
- Is the product or service necessary, optional, or luxury?
- How often do they purchase?
- What is the method of payment (cash, credit cards, installments, advances)?
- How do they use the product or service?
- Does seasonality come into play?
- What prospective customers have you talked to? What was their reaction? Have they seen or tested a prototype of your product or service?
- Does one person make the buying decision or is a committee involved?
- Does the decision have to go through more than one level of approval?
- How long is the decision making process?
- Are the buyer and the user the same?
- How important is personal contact with the customer?

Remember, people make buying decisions. If your business sells to other businesses, you may be selling to a purchasing agent or worse, to a faceless purchasing department.

- Describe how you influence the process and how you benefit the customer.
- How many customers or active accounts do you have? (Depending on the plan you write, and its readership, list your principal customers—citing location, product purchased, and percent of your company's sales—as a supporting document.)
- Point out negatives you have overcome and how you did so.
- What are the effects of product or service introduction on a local, regional, national, or international basis?
- Are there political or regulatory influences? If so, describe them. How will your company qualify for, or pass, statutory requirements? How will it deal with political influences?
- Can you provide verification that customers want or need your product or service? Do so with customer surveys; research data; focus group studies; and articles from magazines, newspapers, trade publications, or book references.

Survey Your Customers

These survey questions help you discover the features your customers or potential customers value most:

- What are the main reasons you bought from us?
- What are the main benefits you receive or expect to receive?
- What sets us apart from our competition?

To identify sources of differentiation in customer service, ask these questions:

- How satisfied are you with our appointment scheduling?
  - our financing?
  - our delivery lead times?
  - our printed materials/documentation?

To find out how buyers perceive your competition, ask:

- Whom do you consider to be our competition?
- What do you like about their product/service? Dislike?
- What do you like about ours? Dislike?

- How do our prices compare?
- Do you shop here or there solely because of price? Location? Service? Warranty?

To understand your customers current and future needs, ask:

- What could we do to make our business worth more to you?
- How have our products/services helped you become more profitable, competitive, or provide better service to you or your customers?

Prepare a Competitive Profile

What percentage of the market can I obtain? Every single product or service has competition. An amazing number of entrepreneurs think they don't have competitors. Frequently the competition may not be direct, however, it's never true to state there is no competition. It may seem absurd, but bread is a competitor to cereal in breakfast food, just as bicycles compete with airplanes in the transportation industry. "I think I'll do without" may be one of your competitors.

Use your competition positively as a teacher and rather than as a negative subject. Remember that a basic positive concept of competition is being responsive to customers. By carefully watching and analyzing your competition, you can better understand what your customers want and how much they're willing to pay. Also, the better you understand your competition, the better job you can do to differentiate your company from the competition.

First, overview the competition from a broad basis. Then provide as much statistical data as possible for each primary competitor. Be sure you are able to back up any narrative opinion with hard, substantiated facts.

Compare each identifiable competitor on

- price, performance, quality, warranties, service, distribution, and features.
- managerial, financial, marketing, and operational strengths and weaknesses.
- trends in their sales, market share, and profitability.

Don't overlook the following:

- What's the general nature of your competition? Are they inadequately or well financed? Are their pricing strategies cut-throat or middle-of-the-road?

- Is new competition entering the industry? How fast? How many?
- How important are national brand names? How about regional, local, or house brands?
- Do you have mail order or catalog competition?
- Can you point out specific weaknesses in your competition?

In most cases, you should be able to classify your competitors into three categories: *dominant, secondary,* or *indirect.* You should also be able to state whether they are publicly or privately held.

A Leading Edge Research Example
● ● ● ● ●

Steve Omar wants to start a school to teach people how to use Microsoft™ office software products. He needs to know how many potential students there are in the Miami/Dade County area of operations.

His research led him to local chamber of commerce data that reveals that 20,000 businesses are classified as small to midsize (1 to 50 employees). The average number of employees is 15. This means that in his business market there are approximately 300,000 potential students.

One final big reminder: *Subjective opinion does not have a place in the market description section.* Use only *facts.* Don't guess in this section. Cite all your facts and note all your sources in a Bibliography. These facts are the foundation for many of your marketing, revenue, and cost assumptions. You can be sure an investor's due diligence process would check them with a fine tooth comb. It's your future at risk—be very sure of your factual information.

Competitive Brief

Here's a simple but effective way to compare competitors. Prepare a list with the top features of your product or service along the left side and the names of the competition along the top. Then rate each feature on a scale of one to ten (ten highest) or "Yes" and "No" to indicate who has what features.

You can also do this same type of comparison for strengths and weaknesses. This was shown in Chapter Six as part of the SWOT test.

	YOUR COMPANY	COMPETITORS				
		1	**2**	**3**	**4**	**5**
Feature One	Y	N	Y	Y	Y	N
Feature Two	Y	Y	N	Y	*	Y
Feature Three	Y	N	N	Y	Y	N
Feature Four	Y	Y	Y	N	N	*
Feature Five	Y	*	Y	N	Y	N

(Codes: Y = Yes, N = No, * = Part of the feature, but not the same)
Company One = ABC Company
Company Two = XYZ Company
Company Three = 123 Company
Company Four = 789 Company
Company Five = your brother-in-law's company

Graphics Sell Your Story

Communication through written reports is a major characteristic of our business society; currently driven by the availability of desk top publishing (DTP). For you to achieve your ultimate goals with your business plan, you depend on your ability to present information in a clear, concise, and persuasive manner. Using charts and other graphic devices are effective ways to complement narrative sections to enhance their power of explanation and effectiveness.

Constantly keep in mind how you can use graphics in your plan. Your choices include photographs; illustrations; bar, column, line and pie/circle charts; flow charts; organization charts; time-line and time/task charts; Gantt and pert charts; maps; plot and floor plans; and schematics. Use a DTP expert to help you design these Leading Edge graphics. Charts, graphs, and tables are effective in competitive comparisons only if they're clear. It's a Leading Edge point.

Project Your Potential

Keep in mind when you're writing this section on your industry, markets, and customers that you have numerous opportunities to stress your product or service advantages regarding quality, price, warranties, service, distribution, and other unique selling points. The more you can show their pertinence to your goals, and the better you can support them with hard data, the better understanding the reader will develop about how terrific your plan is.

12 The Marketing Strategy

By now your business plan covers your products or services, defines your industry and market, and talks about the competition. You are probably starting to feel confident that you really are knowledgeable about your business. It is here in the market strategy section of your plan, that you really demonstrate your company's ability to succeed.

Marketing Strategy is the process of bringing a company to the point where it can make a sale. To develop a marketing strategy, the entrepreneur uses research, personal knowledge, and expert opinions to make good assumptions (See Chapter 7 for more on research and assumptions). These assumptions make it possible to create the products and services people want, place them in front of potential customers, to price them competitively, and make it easy for your customers to buy them.

Marketing is different from sales. Marketing is the strategy and sales are tactics. Where marketing leads customers to your door, sales is the process to take an order *after* the customer is in place. No company succeeds without sales. And sales are generated from a well developed marketing strategy.

Marketing Defined

Marketing is a planning and strategy-based process to satisfy the needs and wants of a customer with one or more defined competitive advantages, at a profit. The key is to satisfy the needs and wants of the customer. If enough people don't want or need your product or service, then all the marketing activities in the world will not make your company successful.

The ideal function of marketing is to make your product or service a substitute for *all* other competitive products or services, and to make *no* competitive products or services substitute for yours. Marketing should increase customer awareness via getting your product or service message to customers effectively through such activities as advertising and publicity. Selling is the solicitation and close.

Leading Edge Marketing Strategy

The Marketing Strategy section of your business plan clearly specifies

- marketing goals—how many units of each product or service you wish to sell, to whom, and when.

- what is to be done by the company, as a whole, to accomplish these goals.

- how each, individual goal is to be achieved; the steps and processes necessary for each.

- who is responsible for achieving each stated goal.

Targeting Your Customers

Your marketing strategy must demonstrate that you have an effective plan to locate prospective customers, capture their interest, motivate them to make a purchase, and can do so at a financial profit. You must clearly state

- how you will to capture the customers' attention.
- what you are going to tell them.
- how you will deliver the message to them.
- how you will actually sell them.

A Market Strategy Exercise

Here's a quick guide to help you develop a marketing and sales strategy.

1. List ten features of your product or service.
2. List five benefits to the buyer/users.
3. List the needs of the buyer which are met by the benefits.
4. List the feelings felt by buyers when their needs are met.
5. List at least five objections you expect to hear.
6. List five alternative ways buyers can fulfill their needs.

Leading Edge Marketing Strategy Objectives

A key point in establishing marketing strategy is to set objectives that maximize your company's resources, capabilities, and capacities. Such objectives include:

- identifying target markets. Aim at the defined characteristics of your customers, versus the market as a whole, with a focused approach.

- choosing specific niches, or carefully defined groups, within target market segments, most likely to desire your products or services.

- gaining early stage entry with technology, knowledge, product, service, or business innovations.

- increasing market share with a carefully thought out, comprehensive approach.

- optimizing profits by using technology, knowledge, and resources efficiently. Also, avoid waste or duplication.

Target Marketing

Marketing to target markets (a defined group or groups) is essential for the new company. You must know who your customers are. The methods to define customer characteristics, market segments, and potential market size were shown in Chapter 4. Another way to define your target markets is by using demographic profiles or other market analysis techniques, which help you focus your promotional and advertising dollars. These methods enable you to penetrate a market segment more rapidly and economically, gaining a larger market share.

These factors may or may not be important to your marketing strategy. If your business involves a commodity, then price, delivery, terms and warranty, and customer service, may be the only factors you can influence. However, psychological factors may be a secret weapon for you.

Take a close look at the lifestyle of your customers, including their business style if you are dealing business to business. Are they seeking a certain image? Do they have common associations (most belong to the same country club or business association or charitable group)? Is there a common vacation destination? Favorite movie, TV program? Common schooling background? In short, is there a "user psychological profile" that you can develop? Are there values or life/business styles that are identified with your customers or markets? Are there outside influences—including political, governmental, or religious—that affect your markets? Incorporate this knowledge in your marketing strategy.

Gaining Market Share

After defining your target market customers, your company must find a way to reach and sell to as many of them as possible. Companies gain market share by offering something different, either with lower prices or with one or more perceived qualities. The list below shows some methods of differentiation. As part of your marketing strategy, you must assess which factors give your company the edge that will gain market share:

Technology innovation	Service innovation
Low marketing costs	Product life cycle at growth stage
Low design and manufacturing costs	Customer perception of high value
Not capital intensive	No good substitutes/Few competitors
High profit potential	No regulatory exposure
Adequate time to exploit market potential	Ability to capture 20 to 40 percent of market
Second stage product/service in development	No seasonal fluctuations

Positioning within Niches

Positioning a product or service determines what particular market niche you are going to fill and how you will fill it via promotion, advertising, and sales—versus your competition. It is especially important for smaller companies and all start-ups. You want to be sure your niche is large enough to allow room for growth but not so large as to attract a lot of competition. It is very difficult to attack big markets.

Positioning might be as simple as location. It may be pricing related. If your company excels in customer service, make it part of your positioning strategy with testimonial letters and strong references. Regardless of how it is done, positioning defines your business as different from competitors because of how well you know and meet your customers' needs.

> ## Leading Edge Positioning: Luminous Paint Products (LPP)
> • • • • •
>
> Luminous Paint Products developed an innovative specialty coating with fiberglass fibers. It applies in fewer steps and lasts longer, but costs more than most industrial paints. While talking with oil industry manufacturers' representatives, LPP's owner learned:
>
> - The separation tanks used in oil fields begin to leak in as little as one year.
>
> - Conventional paints and coatings seldom last long enough to be worth reapplying, which causes an environmental compliance problem for the petroleum industry.
>
> The entrepreneur decides to penetrate the oil industry in this small, unnoticed niche, to avoid head-to-head competition with the larger coating firms. He decides to sell personally to better explain his product's innovations and benefits to potential buyers.

Promotion

Promotion is the process of advancing the information about your product or service to the customer by *any* means. It presents information about your product or service and tells/reminds customers what you offer. The key to successful promotion is to be able to succinctly identify your USP and tell how your USP benefits your customer. Once this is accomplished—which is no small task in itself—you then use paid advertising or publicity to spread your message.

Publicity

Publicity is a separate promotional category that a lot of entrepreneurs ignore when writing their business plan. Publicity is often typecast as "free." However, for those of you who have worked to get publicity, you know it's far from free. It takes a lot of ingenuity—and time—to get this so called free publicity.

The biggest key, and the way you measure your success, is how well you capture the uniqueness of your business and how it benefits your customer.

To get media coverage, you must devise a unique public attention twist or hook that will get an overworked writer or editor to conclude that your story is newsworthy. To get their attention, you create press releases and press kits. You send them to the appropriate media, which means you have to find and maintain a constantly changing database. Mailing hundreds of press releases is far from free, so target your publicity carefully.

If you have been able to put together a dynamite, all-encompassing promotional campaign, describe and give examples in your business plan. This also means you must show dollar amounts and how you will spend them. If you haven't devoted the time, effort, and money to create it yet, then don't talk about it in your business plan. Good promotions capture the investors' attention, while ill-conceived promotional efforts destroy creditability.

Word of mouth publicity has a lot of impact. Good word of mouth results in gaining one new customer at a time. Bad word of mouth will lose ten potential customers. Make word of mouth a positive and rewarding experience for your existing customers, as well as a feedback mechanism. By giving existing customers a brochure on your product or service, it opens the opportunity for you to ask if they are satisfied with your service—which shows you care—and to then ask for referrals. You might even consider a referral reward program by giving them a discount or bonus with every new customer they refer.

Paid Advertising

Paid advertising may be out of reach for early stage entrepreneurs. If you decide to advertise your company, break out the methods used and expenditures for each area chosen. These may include: broadcast media (TV, radio, cable); direct mail (flyers, catalogs, coupons); trade shows, brochures, and flyers (especially for service companies); print media (newspapers, magazines, specialty publications); public relations (feature and news articles); sampling (product samples or coupons); repeat sales; add-ons; co-op advertising; premiums (gifts, sweepstakes, discounts, may be bundled with other companies); the Internet (banner ads); etc. If you use an advertising agency it can prepare this report.

Sales

After you find your customers, your next step is to sell them. As you write your Sales section, you should include how the sales process takes place—pricing, image, packaging, distribution, warranties, and customer relations. Consider the following points:

- Where does the actual sales activity take place? In your business? Over the phone? On a computer? At the customer's, home, office, or plant?
- Do you use an online, in-house, or outside sales force?
- If outside sales, will manufacturers' representatives call on customers, sell in their office or showroom? How do you qualify and select them? Do you use outside telemarketers?
- Is your product line split by products, geographical areas, or specialties?
- What are your distribution levels—direct sales distributors, dealers, manufacturer's representatives, franchises?
- Are salespersons supported by salaries, salary plus commission, commission only, draw and commission, bonuses, or act as independent contractors? Do commissions vary by product or dollar amount? Will your sales personnel have other responsibilities (warranty, service, supplies, add-ons, training)?
- What expenses do you pay or reimburse?
- Do you use incentives (awards, gifts, trips)?
- Do you provide sales training? Who does it, how often, and in what form—meetings, manuals, continuing, seminars, trade shows?
- Who supervises sales—a manager, multiple managers, or district supervisors—and in what way?
- How do/would selling costs as a percentage of revenues vary with more or less sales volume?

For manufacturing companies, include:

- What is current backlog and current shippable backlog? Can shippable backlog be shipped and billed immediately upon completing the manufacturing?
- How many purchase orders are on hand? Do you have letters of commitment?

Explain the Sales Process

Explain the sales process you use. Discuss the following:

- How do you identify prospects?
- How do you generate leads—by advertising, cold calls, referrals, direct solicitation, telemarketing, or purchase mail lists?
- Who makes the contact—initial and follow-up? In person or through e-mail, personal letter, mass mailing, Web site, or other?

- How long is it from when you identify a prospect until you close the sale? How do you track the sales time cycle, motivate and encourage the prospect, and control the process?
- How do you establish sales goals? Do you do this from the top down or bottom up? Do your salespeople set their goals or do you dictate goals to them?
- What assures that a prospect will receive followup on a timely basis? Who does this tracking and what are the reporting systems?

From you to your customer. This might sound like oversimplification to you, but many times it really pays off in your or your reader's understanding if you give a step-by-step explanation of your products' or services' selling processes. Even if you have a retail product sold in thousands of stores all over the world, it is helpful if you show how you get it from your company—or a distributor—to the ultimate customer. Following are some avenues your company may use.

- *Executive selling* is where top management is active in the selling process from beginning to end. They require high skill levels, frequently specialized knowledge, and take a lot of personal effort to develop and secure the sale.
- *In-house sales forces* are supported with expense accounts and work on a commission basis. They usually have in-depth knowledge and are frequently backed by technical or service support.
- *Sales representatives* are independent contractors selling noncompeting lines to a specific industry. They sell almost everything with minimum sales ranging up from $1,000. They are paid by commission. Because they are independent, they understand the costs of selling as they are in business for themselves. Also because they are independent, they can be hard to control.
- *Mass distribution* is for items that are sold in quantity and which usually are priced below $1,000 per item. This may be through retailers, wholesalers, direct mail, and catalogs. Typically, there will be considerable competition.
- *Electronic/online methods* are growing fields that should be considered by the entrepreneur. The process varies widely based on the type of customers, the level of sophistication in market segments, and the current state of telecommunications and transaction protocols in use.

Sales Productivity

When you write your description of the sales process, include the following:

- What are your sales goals (by product units and dollars) over what time frames (daily, weekly, monthly, quarterly, or yearly)?
- What are your sales-per-person?
- How many times do you need to have contact with the customer to make the initial sale? Repeat sales? Supplies? Add-ons?
- What percentage of sales contacts result in a close?
- How is credit checked, who does it, and who approves it?
- Whose responsibility is it to see that an order is filled?
- What are your costs-of-sales?
- Using a chart or map, show how breaking a geographical area (nation, state, city) into territories or regions increases your sales productivity.

Sales Training

If your product or service requires training of salespersons, you should address this fact. Include such areas as what education is required, what previous experience is required, how one should teach selling features and customer benefits, how the selling attitudes and approach of your salespeople to prospective customers can set your product or service apart from the competition.

You should also address the training and sales aids you use. For instance: Do you furnish demonstration units, video and/or audio tapes, specification sheets, brochures, catalogs, samples, reference or testimonial letters, and such other items?

Pricing

The process of setting the price for your products or services can be complicated. Your plan must cover in detail how you determine your pricing. Spend some time with your accountant and learn about the basic pricing principles of full cost, flexible markups, gross margin, and going rate as well as multiple cost, perceived value, expected share, and the various adaptations before you determine your pricing strategies. Investors need to feel that your approach is logical, justified, and will allow an ample return on investment while still leaving room for a margin for error.

Your pricing policy is an important part of your sales strategy. Your business plan should describe your pricing polices with respect to all product or service lines. How sensitive are prices to costs? How sensitive or insensitive are your prices to increases or decreases? As an example, if you increase price by 10 percent, will you lose 20 percent in volume? Obviously, you are seeking a market that is not price sensitive and will allow you large profit margins, at least in the early stages while you develop a leadership position.

If you intend to underprice your competition, you must explain how you will do this and still remain profitable. If your product or service is truly superior to your competition, don't fall into the trap of lower pricing. Lower pricing can only be justified if you can prove large efficiencies and the consequent savings in material costs, manufacturing, distribution, sales, labor costs, service costs, or overhead.

Don't make the mistake of believing that your business is driven by who has the lowest price. Sometimes this is true with commodity items. However, with most businesses the secret is *perceived value*. A lot of customers today consider durability, guarantees, reliability, service, status, delivery, quality, and other factors right along with—if not prior to—lowest price.

Consider the following when composing the pricing segment of your plan:

- How do your competitors determine pricing?
- How do you determine your pricing compared to competition?
- Do you attempt to preserve the same percentage or margin throughout your product line or system?
- How is your pricing influenced by commission levels, especially in distributor or dealer businesses?
- What consideration have you given to volume discounts?
- Do your purchase terms influence pricing? Do you accept credit cards?
- If you sell direct, do you
  - grant a better price than your dealer price?
  - grant a better price if customers pay in advance? Within a certain number of days?
  - offer special pricing to preferred customers?
  - specify your terms: net 30; 2 percent in 10 days; and so on?
- Are there any regulations restricting your pricing policies?
- Can you gain a competitive edge with pricing?
- How do you know customers will pay your price?
- Have you considered your competitors' reaction to your pricing?
- Is your pricing established to assure profits?
- Will your pricing allow you to increase market share?
- Do you have a pricing advantage due to the newness of your product or service?

Image Logo, Product and Packaging Design

How well your product is physically designed is very important to your customer. There are many firms that specialize in the ergonomics of product design. How does it fit in an adult male's hand versus a child's hand? Does the color appeal to feminine tastes? Masculine tastes? Is the case tough enough to withstand hard industrial use? If these types of questions have been addressed in the process of preparing your product for sale, then they rightfully belong in your business plan.

If on the other hand, you have had to confront packaging, especially in all the forms that may be required to comply with some regulatory body (e.g., Luminous Paints needs the U.S. Department of Transportation approval for shipping containers), you should discuss the attention you have paid to this area. Perhaps this is part of the use of proceeds in your financing request.

Stay mindful of the fact that a picture or simple line drawing of your product or packaging is worth several pages of words.

Distribution

When you are describing your distribution, you are describing the manner in which your product, and sometimes a service, are physically transported to the customer. Questions you should answer may be some of the following:

- Is the product shipped by U.S. mail, delivery service, or trucking shipper?
- Is the physical shipping provided by a manufacturers' representative, dealer or drop-shipped from your facility?
- Who pays the shipping costs? From where to where (e.g., door-to-door, city-to-city)?
- Are there intermediaries in your distribution channel such as retailers, wholesalers, or jobbers? How do they effect distribution?
- Do you need to address other functions of your distribution such as transportation, storage, direct delivery, installation, or immediate service?
- If you intend to run a service business:
  - Do you provide in-home, in-shop, in-office, or in-business service?
  - Do you make house calls? If so, how are mileage costs handled? What is your response time? Are customer's billed for travel time?
  - Do you have back-up vehicles (in case of breakdown)?

Customer Service

Today, customer service has to be an integrated part of your business. It has to start at the top and permeate throughout your whole company. If you haven't built that understanding into your total approach to your business, you won't get funded or prove successful. A defined service policy assures the reader that management is conscious of its responsibility to remedy problems that may be associated with their product or service. Address these questions in your plan:

- What customer service is required?
- What service does the market expect?
- What continuing service has to be provided?
- How will you provide the services?
- How about return policy and money back or prorated guarantees?

Warranty

For most product companies and some service firms, warranties or service policies are important to the customer's buying decision. If this is true for your company, you need to describe your methods of handling follow-ups. Describe the industry standards, how your company compares, and if yours are better, how this is a selling point. If you have a warranty or service fulfillment obligation, describe the method of handling it; the facilities and personnel needed; service or repair centers or arrangements; and arrangements with dealers, distributors, and outside contractors. Also include information pertaining to charges connected with fulfillment and whether service will be profitable or break even.

Other Markets

Will you be moving into new markets? Address this possibility by asking the following questions:

- Will you be developing new markets by expanding geographically and finding new uses for existing products or service applications?
- Will you subcontract to efficiently utilize production capacity or service delivery?
- Will you acquire another company or store/facility in another state/city/neighborhood?
- Do you have any existing or contemplated licensing agreements?
- Do you have franchise potential?
- Do you currently have or are you developing plans for international marketing?
- Are you developing new products for new markets?

Projections

Marketing projections are similar to your financial projections (discussed in Chapter 14). However, your market projection concern is to present details on units of volume as opposed to dollar amounts. You'll need to do these over a three to five year basis by showing the first year month by month, the second and third year quarterly, and the fourth and fifth year, in annual figures. It doesn't hurt to show both units or department figures. This reinforces the development of your total revenues. The dollar figures are not necessary as you will be recapping these in the financial section.

The charts you use can be very simple or extremely complex depending upon your business. If you have a number of product lines or departments, you have a challenge in breaking each one out individually. You can also show developing sales programs by breaking out sales by persons, dealer, distributor, or regions. You can further elaborate by showing percentages of market share or penetration. This is an ideal place to use graphs. Don't forget to back up your market projections with solid assumptions of how you will achieve each goal.

Strategies—A Final Word

We've covered a lot of ideas and methods that have to be considered in this section on marketing strategies. However, when implementing strategies, keep one word uppermost in your mind: *clear*. If your strategy cannot be explained in clear, simple words, go back and try again. If your business plan readers don't understand your marketing strategy, you won't get the dollars.

In this complex but important section, you should have described

- the message you are sending to your customers and prospective clients.
- how you are positioning your company and its products or services.
- the marketing methods and vehicles you are using.
- your sales force, your strategy, and the procedures you have in place to assure sales success.

13

The Leading Edge Management Team

It is well documented that the skills and experience of the management team have more to do with the success of a company than the product or service. Business plan reviewers are seeking a sense of the management team's strengths and implied weaknesses to give them a better understanding of the tasks and risks involved, while reviewing the balance of the plan.

For Smaller Companies

If your company is a small concern with just one or two principals, you must approach the management section with a little different emphasis. Equity investors or debt lenders need and want to know more about you. Whether you are looking for investment capital or not, it is suggested that you supply this information in the form of a longer narrative that addresses the following broad points:

- What is your business background, especially as it relates to the type of business you're proposing?
- What direct management experience do you have that is applicable to this new position?
- What other experiences show your management and team leader skills, such as civic or religious organizations in which you participate.
- What are your personal motives related to the company and what special interests or abilities will be beneficial to running it?
- Discuss your health status.
- Disclose your personal financial status in the form of a personal balance sheet as well as those of other key equity holders.

- Cite your areas of responsibility, to whom and how you will delegate or divide duties, and show how you will address the weak spots.
- If you're a partnership, be sure to describe the division of responsibilities, why each partner is best suited for her particular area, and how they complement each other.
- Describe the areas where you lack the specific background, competence, expertise, qualifications, or skills, and explain how the company will overcome this issue.

Independent Contractors

Many Leading Edge entrepreneurs depend on a variety of independent contractors. It is important that you know the laws that are applicable for your state as well as the rules and regulations that the IRS applies to accounting for independent contractors. State information can be obtained from your Secretary of State's office.

Getting Intimate with the Management Team Requirements

Because entrepreneurs come with varying talents, personalities, skill areas, and adaptability, the blend and unique fit among the founders is most important. The objective is to blend the talents of the entrepreneur with the capabilities of equally talented and committed partners and subordinates. If they can work well together and together seize and execute the opportunity, the chances for success are dramatically improved.

The functions of a management team differ for different companies, depending on the nature of the company. For instance, the owner of a Leading Edge company may be the only initial employee, but it will be more successful if she has access to other people who can counsel her in her areas of weakness. She may be good at sales but lousy at accounting, or good at seeking out the best suppliers but terrible at figuring out the best ways to ship.

In another example, a company that subcontracts all of its manufacturing most likely will not need a production manager; though it may need a quality control expert. Specific management abilities function in specific designated areas. Following is a general list of guidelines, qualifications, and fundamentals outlining abilities by various members of a full management team for a variety of companies. How do these ideal management requirements fit your Leading Edge enterprise?

Administration and General Management

- *Leadership.* Ability to form a vision and motivate others.
- *Communication.* Ability to communicate clearly and effectively to all parties and the public in both written and oral form.
- *Making decisions.* Ability to take input from the team and implement changes.
- *Negotiating.* Ability to solicit recommendations from all sides, balance opinions, and achieve consensus for mutual benefit.
- *Planning.* Ability to identify obstacles, establish attainable goals, and develop and implement action plans.
- *Problem solving.* Ability to gather and analyze facts, anticipate and avoid trouble, implement solutions effectively, and follow up thoroughly and in a timely fashion.
- *Project and task management.* Ability to properly define and set goals, organize participants, and monitor a project to completion.

Operations Management

- *Inventory and quality control.* Ability to establish suitable inspection standards, maintain accuracy, and set realistic dollar benchmarks for raw, in-process, and finished goods.
- *Manufacturing.* Demonstrated experience in the process; openness to continuing improvement of techniques; managing people power, machinery, time costs, and quality needs of the customer.
- *Purchasing.* Ability to seek out the most appropriate sources and suppliers; consider cost, delivery time, and quality; and to effectively negotiate contracts and manage flow; all while balancing current need and dollar resources.

Financial Management

- *Capital raising.* Ability to determine the best approach, structure debt/equity and short- versus long-term financials, and familiarity with sources.
- *Money controls.* Ability to design, implement, and monitor all money management; and to set up systems for overall and individual projects.
- *Ratios applications.* Ability to produce detailed pro formas and actual statements for profit and loss (P&L), cash flow, and balance sheets; and to analyze and monitor all financial areas.

Marketing Management

- *Evaluation and research.* Ability to conduct thorough studies using proper demographics, and to interpret and analyze the results in structuring viable territories and sales potential.
- *Planning.* Ability to provide promotion, advertising, and sales programs that are effective with and for sales representatives and distributors.
- *Product continuation.* Ability to determine service and spare parts requirements, track customer complaints, and supervise the setup and management of the service organization.
- *Product distribution.* Ability to manage and supervise product flow from manufacturing through the channels of distribution to the end user, with attention to costs, scheduling, and planning techniques.
- *Support.* Ability to obtain market share by organizing, supervising, and most important, motivating a sales force.

Research and Development, Engineering and Technical Management

- *Research.* Ability to distinguish between basic and applied research, keeping a bottom-line balance.
- *Networking.* Ability to stay current and apply software, hardware, and network and telecommunications technology to company processes.
- *Engineering.* Ability to supervise the final design through engineering, testing, and manufacturing.
- *Development.* Ability to guide product development so that a product is introduced on time, within budget, and meets the customers' basic needs.

Personnel Management

- *Conflict.* Ability to confront differences openly and use teamwork to determine resolution.
- *Criticism.* Ability to receive feedback without becoming defensive; and to provide constructive criticism.
- *Culture.* Ability to create an atmosphere and attitude conducive to high performance, and to reward either verbally or monetarily work well done.
- *Development.* Ability to select and coach subordinates and pass this ability on to peers.
- *Help.* Ability to determine situations where help is needed.
- *Listening.* Ability to listen without prejudging, hear the message, and make effective decisions.

Legal Management

- *Contracts.* Experienced in, and knowledgeable about, the broad procedures and structure for government regulation and commercial law, including warranty, default, and incentives.
- *Corporate.* Experienced in and knowledgeable about the intricacies of incorporation, leases, distribution, and patents.
- *Compliance.* Experience in compliance with local, state, federal, and if necessary, international regulations concerning all aspects of employment and business operations.

These lists cover the basic qualifications, abilities, and characteristics the entrepreneur should take into account when assembling a full management team. Common to all the management disciplines are the following five basic management functions.

Five Basic Management Functions

It's the entrepreneurs' responsibility to ascertain if their prospective team leaders are proficient in the following five basic management functions:

1. *Setting objectives* in clear, concise terms.
2. *Setting an organization* structure which entails analysis and classification of work.
3. *Communication* with, and motivation of, people. This is essential because in the final analysis it is the people who get the job done. How well they do it depends on the quality of the communication and degree of motivation.
4. *Follow-up,* measuring of performance and results.
5. *Development* of good people, in present jobs as well as in anticipation of future advancement.

With the qualifications and functions defined, the Leading Edge entrepreneur can turn to the tasks of identifying and putting together a team. When this is accomplished, the next task is to properly portray the qualities of the team to the business plan reader.

Defining Your Management Team

Keeping in mind that we are addressing a Leading Edge business that aspires to grow into a major contender in its industry, we are presenting the following as a guide to the contents of a full-blown business plan.

Your Leading Edge plan will probably have much less management detail and substance. However, you need to give thought to the makeup of a larger organization when considering the expanding requirements for your management team.

Ideally, this section of your plan should cover career highlights, accomplishments, positions held, and emphasis on good performance records for all the management people in your company. Your concern is not to present detailed resumes, these should be included as exhibits in your supporting documents section. You should present a narrative on each individual that addresses the following key points: Name, age, position—then a few lines of career and educational highlights focusing on past accomplishments that demonstrate ability to perform for the company. When applicable, note when any of these individuals have worked together before.

Top Management

These are most likely the officers of your company (or, if you are a start-up sole proprietor, it would obviously be only yourself and/or maybe your spouse). Note if they are founders and if they are also on your board of directors. Besides the key points mentioned above, briefly describe the duties and responsibilities of each top management person.

Add a note if any top management personnel vacancies will be filled. If you have not identified an individual, then present the job qualifications which you will be seeking. Many business plan reviewers are used to seeing plans where a complete team is not in place; and many times, they may know a good candidate for you.

Support Professionals

Leading Edge companies routinely use outside contractors to fill important, or technical, job functions where larger firms would have employees. If you intend to use outside support professionals to fill the gaps in your management team, cite this expertise and note how it will help you gain advantages in your business.

This is also the area where you should list your other outside professionals such as accountants and attorneys. You may have multiples of these such as a bookkeeping service, payroll service, and a CPA. Multiples also may apply to your legal needs if your company has some specialty area or is involved in patenting products. Each of these professionals should be listed and brief descriptions of their value are suitable. Don't forget advertising, bankers, and insurance agents.

Also give consideration to the following points:

- If a stock option or other management incentive plan is in place, provide an outline.
- Show that references are available.
- Discuss how innovation and creativity is encouraged and supported.
- What key personnel life insurance is in place or will be purchased?
- Are employment contracts in place?
- Are there any consulting contracts (proposed) between the company and any members of management, shareholders, or outside consultants?

A Leading Edge Example
• • • • •

Computer Training Services, Inc. (CTS)

Computer Training Services, Inc. will offer classes in software use. In two years it intends to have three full-time instructors, including the owner.

- The owner decides to bring in two experienced software teachers with whom he has worked before. Each begins on a part-time basis, being paid on a per-class basis. As an employment incentive, he offers each teacher equity for performing their duties satisfactorily.
- He obtains three professional advisers, including a teacher from the local community college, and an officer at a local bank.

Board of Directors

List the members of your board of directors (if applicable), using short resumes (biographies) and emphasize their major contributions to the company. It is not unusual, if you're seeking financing, that you allow a representative of your financing sources to sit on the board. Frequently, when asking for large amounts of investment capital, outside investors will insist on one or more board seats and will bring expertise along with their money. You may wish to discuss your philosophy as to the size and composition of your board (number of inside versus outside seats).

Board of Advisers

It is rare that a sole entrepreneur has the breadth and depth of knowledge to cover all the functions and tasks of the new company, even if the entrepreneur has previous industry experience. Things change too quickly to keep up with innovation and still run a business. An entrepreneur without prior business experience is going to need even more advice.

Well-chosen advisers add prestige and credibility to an entrepreneurial company, especially when it comes to fund raising. They are experts in various fields where the entrepreneur is not. Their function is to consult with the entrepreneur, directors, and company management on technical, management, economic, and other matters that affect the company.

The board of advisers is not set up as a committee of the board, although in some corporate structures it is considered to be one. The advisers are appointed by the board of directors, but they are separate from the board. In most companies, advisers may not be officers, directors, or employees of the company.

A Leading Edge Example
• • • • •
Construction Delivery Corporation (CDC)

Construction Delivery Corporation wants to build a sophisticated blueprint room, offering electronic, just-in-time delivery on the Internet, to compete with conventional construction bid rooms. The entrepreneur needs help to build, test, maintain, and improve the application; cover an array of legal requirements; find corporations and government entities willing to list their blueprints; and to publicize and sell the service to industry associations, contractors, suppliers, and other vendors.

- The owner decides these functions are so important that he develops seven board of directors seats for the various specialties.

- He enlists three professional advisers.

- He knows he is on the hunt for more.

It should be noted, too, that members of the board of advisers serve at the pleasure of the board of directors and receive compensation as determined by the board, often only in the form of consulting fees. They also are provided with liability indemnification by the company.

There are no requirements for formal group meetings by the board of advisers and, in fact, it's not unusual that they never meet as a group. Individual members of the board of advisers are consulted in their areas of expertise as necessary.

Organization Chart

If you hope to grow a larger organization, furnish an organization chart. Sometimes it's helpful to have several charts that depict the initial group and the expanded organization in years three and five.

	Board of Directors	
	President	
Engineering		Personnel
Vice President	Treasurer-CFO	Vice President
Marketing		Production
Sales Manager A		Plant A
Sales Manager B		Plant B

Management Remuneration

Compile a simple compensation table that shows names/positions, salary and bonus (if applicable), fee arrangements, commissions, profit sharing, stock options, and existing equity interests for every officer.

Name	Position	Remuneration	Stock Owned (Options)
John Smith	President, CEO	$80,000[1]	120,000 shares
To be named	Executive VP, COO	$75,000[4]	10,000 options
John Smith, Jr.	VP, Secretary	$75,000[1]	120,000 shares
Joan Smith	VP Marketing	$50,000[2]	(30,000 shares)
Joanne Smith	VP Engineering	$60,000[3]	
Jack Smith	Treasurer, CFO	$55,000[3]	

[1] Founder, existing equity, holds stock options
[2] Existing equity, bonus and commission
[3] Bonus
[4] Bonus, stock options

Human Resources Management

The area of human resource management can be very critical in all sizes of companies. If you are operating a company that is on a fast-track growth plan, improper hiring practices can be disastrous. This is from both a legal standpoint, and for the company's success. Every new hire costs the company money for the first three months, allows the company to break even the next three, and won't become profitable until after the first six months. Some think that in large companies, these time periods double; that's one year before you start to realize profit potential from a new hire.

Because of these facts, it is important that you demonstrate in your business plan that you have a good grasp of the personnel side of your company. Think about the appropriate points listed below when you write this section:

- What training is required, who will do it, and at what costs in both time and money?
- Will you be hiring salaried or hourly workers?
- What fringe benefits will you provide?
- Will you need full- or part-time employees?
- What about paying overtime?
- What skills will you be hiring for and are they immediately available at rates you can afford?
- Define your personnel needs now and in the future (in months, quarters, or years, as appropriate).

Resume Hint

Recognizing that you have put hundreds of hours into conceiving and writing this plan. There is one other area where you can make your plan stand out from 75 percent of all the others. Retype all resumes in the same general format. It really looks sloppy to turn to the Appendix and see eight resumes, each one copied from an original and each in a different format. It's a couple more hours that really make a difference in making your plan look professional.

Summary

Your primary challenge in this section is to present a discussion of the skills of your management team, those both inside and outside the company. Be sure that all the information you present is accurate. This is the place to be direct and honest.

14

The Financials

As detailed in this chapter, a company's financials are a set of documents that present a historical, current, and projected overview of key numbers pertinent to the business plan. These numbers are the backbone of a company's operations, and reviewed by all investors.

Few business plans treat this section properly. This is especially true in today's environment of computer generated financial statements. Everyone gets fascinated with gobs of computer generated spreadsheets feeling that quantity will be seen as quality. For Leading Edge companies, this is a completely unneeded exercise. If you have followed the steps outlined earlier in this book, you conducted some basic financial feasibility/research studies. These provide the basis for the assumptions and numbers you will be working with in your plan's financial section.

Smaller companies have less need for complicated financial presentations. Because the business is smaller in all areas—e.g., number of employees, amount of sales, inventories, assets, accounts receivable—the financials can be simpler in presentation. However, the less complicated nature does not mean that the basic financial factors should be ignored.

This chapter presents a lot of food-for-thought information. The start-up Leading Edge company should review the full section and then determine what is needed for their size project. The sample plans in this chapter will prove good guides for small Leading Edge companies, as opposed to the expansive financial plans needed for companies seeking large amounts of financing.

Summarize before You Start

Open this section with a brief paragraph or two of overview narrative about your financial plan. Sometimes this can be very brief, simply stating that it is a sole proprietorship and that the one or two pages supply thebasic projections and assumptions.

A Leading Edge Note to Entrepreneurs

Your financial sections, and the facts and assumptions that underlie them, are the true demonstration that your company can operate at a profit, and pay back its investment in a reasonable time. If your finances do not clearly match your expectations, then you need to go back and

- improve your research;

- improve your assumptions;

- build a better, measurable system to run the company; or

- consider another business.

In more complex presentations, summarize projections that address several of the key areas including sales, expenses, net income, and total growth in assets and net worth. This narrative is then followed by a summary projection chart that covers three to five years (or whatever period you are compiling projections for) and the following key categories:

- From your income statements: sales, cost of goods, gross income, expenses, and net income
- From your balance sheet: assets, liabilities, and net worth
- From your corporation records: you may want to show how these pro forma figures translate into per share figures (discussed later in this chapter)

The Offer

If you are seeking debt or equity financing, the second step in the financial section is to present an offer to the potential investor. Many business plan writers fail to do this. If they get up the courage to make an offer, they bury it in the last part of the plan, presumably because they want to build the pitch to justify their offer.

The correct way to approach this subject is to come right out and state that you are seeking X amount of debt, to be repaid over X period of time, offering X percent interest, *or* X amount of equity by selling X number of shares of stock at X price per share which constitutes X percent of the company. If you intend to start a limited liability company (LLC), then state you are offering X percent of the company and the rest of your terms. The prospective financing source is interested in knowing the terms of your offer while they are analyzing the facts presented in your plan.

For the entrepreneur, this is a good time to think about growth and how you might finance it. Or you might use this opportunity for role playing by asking an associate or an adviser what she or he would want in return for an investment or a loan to the company. At the very least you end up with some idea of the company's initial value, can be quite useful before making a personal investment decision. You also get an idea of the quality of your presentation.

Use of Proceeds

Once you have summarized your financials and presented your offer, the third step is to broadly discuss your use of proceeds. This section previews how many dollars you need and what you'll spend them on. It should list and describe the amounts, all in broad categories. Do not use a detailed listing of all the equipment you intend to purchase, just list "equipment" or "office equipment" or "shop equipment." You should provide the details later on. The same for the other broad categories in your use of proceeds. For now, just generalize, and then provide details later in this section, in the body of the plan, or in the Appendix.

Most emerging growth companies require multiple stages of financing, including both debt and equity. Start-up plans need to detail start-up use of proceeds and then generalize on the additional stages.

The Exit

Step four in your initial section on financing is to present your exit plan—how the investor will get their money back. When you incur debt, your lender expects to get its money back plus a profit (interest). Lenders judge your plan on the company's ability to repay the debt with interest on time. Your narrative comment here can be something to the effect that your cash flow studies indicate the full amount of debt can be repaid within X amount of time.

For equity investors, it's a different story. They are owners in your company and they also expect to earn a profit on their investment. Some investors expect a return in the form of dividends. Others may be investing for the day you sell out, expecting a long-term appreciation on their investment. While others, like venture capitalist or professional private investors, expect you to have an exit or harvest plan. They want you to liquidate their investment in the form of cash or tradeable public stock.

All investors should be concerned as to how they are going to get their money out, but sophisticated equity investors won't even look at your plan unless you can tell them up-front what your exit strategy is and convince them that the exit is viable. Unless you are operating a small company that is going to provide your primary, if not sole, source of income, you should also be concerned about how you're going to get your money back.

Delving into the Details

If you're going to prepare a more complex financial section, you can begin furnishing the details here. Keep these points in mind:

- Refrain from ambiguous, unsubstantiated statements like "sales will grow rapidly."
- You must be prepared to live with the numbers you set forth, remembering that you will be judged by them. The investor is buying into your deal from these numbers. The investor will pull your plan out time and time again as the months and years roll by. If you aren't realistic in your original projections, you'll have to spend a lot of time explaining why you missed your numbers.

Capitalization

When considering a company's capitalization, the first item the investor needs to know is who currently owns what percentage of your company. You should present the company's current *equity* capital structure (who owns how much) as well as future plans.

- If you are a sole proprietorship, partnership, or a closely held private corporation, list all owners or shareholders (and the percentages they hold). For any who hold 5 percent or more that aren't officers/directors, note their connection to the company.
- If you're a corporation:
  - Show total authorized common/preferred stock.

- Show total outstanding common/preferred stock.
- Describe principle terms, including voting rights, dividend payments, and conversion terms of preferred stock.
- List shareholders of 5 percent or more.
- For the debt side:
  - Provide a list of lenders or note holders with terms of the loan (initial date, amount, length of term, date of maturity, interest percentages, and note any that are subordinated).
  - If you have or have had lines of credit, list these (current and past five years, with whom, amount, terms).

Historical Financials

If you are an existing Leading Edge company seeking to expand, you should provide past financial statements of income and balance sheets for the last three years. Note if there have been any IRS audits and the results, and also note that tax returns are available. Also note if all taxes have been paid, and if you have any existing tax disputes.

Current Financials

Providing current financials is a must, even for start-up companies; even if the company has just been formed and there have been no significant accounting transactions. You always want to provide the latest possible information. Try to get data from within a month of the date on your plan. If this is not possible, provide financials to the latest quarter. Current financials should include an income statement and balance sheet, as well as any accounting notes.

Use Their Forms

If you are seeking debt financing from a particular source—such as your bank, an SBA loan, or other specific debt provider, it is advisable that you inquire if they have a loan package that they would prefer you to submit. Many financial institutions have these packages of forms that they prefer all loan applicants to use.

The advantage to them is that they are familiar with the layout and makeup of these forms and it makes it easier and quicker for them to process. An advantage for you is that you know exactly what information they are seeking, which saves you a lot of time and trouble, avoiding gathering unneeded information.

However, if you feel that you have some data that supports your request and will be helpful in persuading a lender to endorse your project, by all means submit it along with their package. Almost all lenders love to have a lot of paperwork in their files to back up their decision making process.

Detailed Financial Projections

At this point, you're about to let the financing source gaze into your crystal ball by furnishing your projected financial results. For equity investors, these are the bases that support the value of your company and are keys to determine how much of the company to give up in exchange for the funding you are requesting.

Generally, business plans should contain projections for five years. These should be presented month by month for the first year, quarterly for the second and third years, and yearly thereafter.

Various surveys and studies conducted among professional investors such as venture capitalists, investment bankers and commercial bankers, have shown that few financial projections are ever met as they are originally proposed. This would lead one to wonder "why go to all the trouble?"

The answer to that is that *you need to go through the thought process of putting together a detailed financial study by running your company on paper.* You need to demonstrate that all the information and conclusions you make in your plan will work with the numbers. The results of all your strategy development and planning are the financial projections.

Keep in mind that if you have done a good job in presenting your plan thus far, an investor will go over your projections with the proverbial fine tooth comb. If you have holes in this section, they will be discovered, and could kill the deal. The biggest mistake made in today's world of computerized spreadsheets is to simply "plug in" figures. Resist the urge to put in percentage plug figures; e.g., specifying advertising as a percent of sales. This immediately alerts a sophisticated investor that you haven't thought through the advertising expenditure process.

To carry this example further, think about spending dollars on advertising. These types of dollars are usually spent before you receive the benefit, sometimes months before. Many industry publications in which you may advertise have a two- to four-month lead-time. The actual sales may start appearing a month after the publication. Also, think about how seasonality affects an advertising program. Or how about a month when you do a trade show? Or what if you are doing a coupon book or special discount program? These examples show why it looks strange on a spreadsheet to see advertising plugged in as 3 percent of a month's sales revenues as a constant figure throughout a one- to five-year projection.

The point is that all expenses have variables and each of your expense categories must be thought through on a month-by-month basis before you plug them into your computerized spreadsheet. Here's another example that really stands out when a financial source is reviewing a cash flow projection. Say you intend to add several people to your administrative staff. If they are scheduled to come on board in month eight, will you have to spend some extra dollars in month seven to buy some new desks and chairs? And with this addition of more staff, will your office supply expenses increase in month nine? Or if one of these is a traveling salesperson, will you need to provide for additional travel expenses in month ten after they have had home office training? Again, point is that each expense item needs to be carefully planned and documented in your projections.

Be Realistic

Watch out for spreadsheets that get out of hand. These are the spreadsheets that show a respectable 5 percent after-tax net profit the first year, and than because the following year figures are plugged, ends up showing 5 percent yearly increases that amount to a total 25 percent net profit in the fifth year. This looks unreal to an investor who knows that in your industry—which has been around for 50 years—no one has ever exceeded 18 percent after-tax profits. For the industry-knowledgeable, sophisticated business plan reader, a red flag goes up and immediately destroys any creditability you have worked so hard to build in the rest of your plan.

The opposite side of being realistic goes back to customizing your plan for the financial source for which you're aiming. Traditional institutional venture capital funds aren't the least bit interested in looking at projects that will return only 15 percent on their investment or obtain a few million in revenues by the fifth year.

Generally speaking, for your project to be of interest to a venture capital firm, your funding need should be at least a half a million dollars, your annual sales revenue should be a minimum of $20 million within five years, and your projected returns should approach 30 percent *compounded annually*. To justify venture capital investment, your project has to be super high-growth and provide outrageous returns. Save yourself a lot of time, effort, and money—not to mention a great amount of emotional frustration—by being realistic throughout the business planning process. This includes the rationale as to where and how you intend to seek funding.

The point is, always step back and review financial projections and their results with reality questions. Does this seem realistic? Am I sure this is practical, achievable, and real life? Does it make sense and are the conclusions logical? Junk in projections equals junk out, which leads to no financing or a busted company dream.

Assumptions

The second biggest mistake that most entrepreneurs make in furnishing their financial projections is not furnishing solid, detailed assumptions to back up their figures. A total lack of, or incomplete or poorly conceived assumptions, is an immediate tip-off that the entrepreneur is not very savvy.

Assumptions are the backbone, the foundation, of believability for your financial projections. They disclose what the entrepreneur assumed in order to arrive at the numbers. Here are several oversimplified examples:

- Under the Sales category in your Income Statement, you need to state that your assumption is that each salesperson is able to sell X number of units, or dollars, per month.
- Under the Cost of Goods category in your Income Statement, you need to state that according to your calculations (backed-up with facts), that when you reach certain predetermined volume levels, that your costs for parts or supplies will decrease by whatever specified amounts or percentages.
- Under the Expense categories in your Income Statement, you have numerous categories that require full explanations of your assumptions, such as salaries (how much to what individuals), or benefits (what benefits you are furnishing to what individuals). Another expense area is rent—how many square feet at what cost per square foot including what services (janitorial, snow removal, etc.); or utilities, including what variables depending on what demand; or phone expense, detailing how much long distance (do you have an 800 number?).

As you can begin to see, the assumption sections of your financials can go on seemingly forever. You have to use some discretion or you'll end up with 30 pages of details backing up six pages of projections. Your challenge is to present enough assumption detail to make the reader comfortable that you have carefully thought through these back-up figures. Another way to do this is to make sure the reader can see clearly how you calculated the various items. It may be practical to note that more detailed assumptions are available upon request, but do not say this unless you are prepared to deliver.

WARNING! Projections

The financial projection parts of any business plan require many "guesstimates" and forward looking assumptions on the part of the management team. Consequently, this leaves the team open for many near-hits and most times an awful lot of crystal ball gazing strikeouts. Therefore, it's important that you recognize this and acknowledge your vulnerability by adding disclaimers to all your projections. You should check with your attorney in the event she or he has a favorite example such as the following:

> The financial projections contained herein reflect management judgments based on the most likely set of circumstances and conditions and assume the successful completion of the proposed financing. Results may vary considerably and it is extremely unlikely that all events will, in fact, occur as assumed.

Income Statement Projections—with Units

These are also commonly referred to as *Profit and Loss (P&L) Statements.* An income statement summarizes the revenues and expenses for a given accounting period—monthly, quarterly, year-to-date, or annually. If your business is built around a product line (one plus a limited number of versions of a type of product), you should include the number of units sold for each product in your income projections.

For example, say you manufacture refrigerators in three different sizes. In month one, show that you intend to sell ten of Model A, fifteen of Model B, and six of Model C. Footnote the amount of what each model sells for and then show the progression of the number of sales each month in the first year. Obviously if you intend to introduce a line of two different models of stoves in the second year, you will indicate these in the same way. By doing this, the reader has a better sense of the reality involved in your thinking as to how you see the ongoing revenue stream developing.

If your business is in retail, you can show this same logical progression of sales development by replacing the units designation with various departments. For a service company, it may be possible for you to show this as various service areas.

With the unit concept in mind, the other categories you need to show in your Income Statement section are:

Item
Sales Revenues
  Sales Allowances
Cost of Sales:
  Material
  Labor
  Overhead
    Total
Gross Margin (Total Sales less the Cost of Sales)
Operating Expenses:
  Marketing/Selling Costs
    Salaries/Commissions
    Advertising
    Other
  Research and Development
  General and Administrative
  Depreciation/Amortization
    Total
Income (Loss) before Taxes
Taxes on Income
Net Income (Loss)

Don't forget that you need back-up detail to support this income statement including assumptions and perhaps some operational footnotes. This section is also a dynamite place to display your spreadsheet computer skills by providing figures for the various categories calculated as a percentage of sales.

Cash Flow Projections (The Most Important Financial Statement)

Cash flow projections are the most important projection because they detail the anticipated cash inflow and outflow (the same as a budget). It allows you to identify when cash is expected to be received and when you expect to pay your bills.

In practice, cash flow statements are used to anticipate problems. They project your actual cash positions in advance and allow the management team to coordinate their borrowing, debt repayment, and other critical capital position decision making items. Cash flow projections, like income statements, should be shown for the first year month by month, second and third years quarterly, and forth and fifth years, annually.

The categories to be shown in your cash flow statements are similar to the P&L categories, but include a beginning and ending cash balance (see the sample plans for simple, combined P&L and cash flows). A detailed cash flow projection forecasts the need for additional capital or demand for peak requirements in working capital for seasonal fluctuations, inventory build-up, high growth rates, or a variety of other cash flow demands.

Balance Sheet Pro Formas

In its simple mathematical form, the balance sheet relationship is assets minus liabilities equals net worth. Stated another way, if you take anything and everything the company owns of monetary value (assets), subtract everything the company owes to others (liabilities), and what you have left is the net worth (capital) of the company.

Balance sheets are like taking a photograph of your company's financial condition at a particular moment in time. It shows what your company owns and owes and how much it is worth on a certain date. It lists the assets required to support your company and the liabilities show how these assets are financed.

Under normal operating conditions, you would draw up a balance sheet on a monthly, quarterly, and annual basis. Annual presentations are usually sufficient for pro formas. The approach should conform with acceptable accounting practices as investors use the balance sheets to evaluate the appreciation of the company's assets. If you're not familiar with what is considered acceptable, study other well known company financials (public company financials are readily available in their annual reports), or better yet, ask your accountants. They will be glad to assist you with examples and pass along some additional knowledge.

The following are the basic categories that are commonly included in balance sheet pro formas:

ASSETS:
  Current Assets
    Cash
    Investments
    Accounts Receivable
      (Less allowance for doubtful accounts)
    Notes Receivable
    Inventory
    Prepaid Expenses
      Total Current Assets
  Fixed Assets

Land
Buildings
Equipment
    Total Fixed Assets
Other Assets
TOTAL ASSETS

LIABILITIES and SHAREHOLDERS' EQUITY:
    Current Liabilities
    Short-Term Debt
    Accounts Payable
    Taxes Payable
    Income Taxes Payable
    Accrued Liabilities
        Total Current Liabilities
    Long-Term Debt
    Shareholders' Earnings (Deficit)
        TOTAL
    TOTAL LIABILITIES and SHAREHOLDERS' EQUITY

Breakeven Analysis

A breakeven chart is sometimes used for new or start-up ventures to determine at what point the company's total sales equal total costs. By doing a breakeven, you show a prospective financing source that you are aware of how much money you need to get or keep your company going. An entrepreneur also can use a breakeven analysis to chart positive cash flow for a prospective new product or service. If you don't understand the process of constructing a breakeven analysis, consult your accountant.

Supplemental Financial Information

This is an area where you are the best judge of what supplemental information, if any, should be supplied. You may wish to include discussions on tax effects of previous or contemplated financing, thoughts on limited partnerships, joint ventures, bank and credit arrangements, long-term debt, existing debt that can be converted to equity, etc.

It also may be helpful if you provide some industry averages for investor comparison to your projections. These can be obtained from such sources as trade associations, various bank reference books, or from publications that compile information on publicly held companies in your industry. These averages are useful as back-up or to indicate exceptions in your plan for above- or below-averages in areas such as research and development, excess marketing expenses, salaries and compensation, or extraordinary capital expenditures.

Detailed Use of Proceeds—Sources and Application of Funds

Here's an added financial exhibit that will win you points with any financing source. It's very valuable when you are using combinations of debt and equity to provide those with an investment interest a clear picture of the interrelationships of your financing.

SOURCES

Building/Property Mortgage Loan		$xx,xxx
Term Loan(s)		$xx,xxx
Line of Credit		$xx,xxx
SBA Loan		$xx,xxx
New Equity Investment	$xx,xxx	
TOTAL		$xx,xxx

APPLICATIONS

Purchase Property		$xx,xxx
New Equipment	$xx,xxx	
Refurbished Equipment	$xx,xxx	
Office Improvements		$xx,xxx
Inventory Additions		$xx,xxx
Working Capital		$xx,xxx
TOTAL		$xx,xxx

Polishing Your Financial Strut

Most financing sources are seeking projects where the product or service is innovative or unique, those that find a need and fill it. However, when it comes to the financial section, they are looking for the tried and true in presentation form. Don't get fancy or attempt to develop new ways to present your financial information.

Simply follow the formats presented above. Start with an overview and then present the details, as appropriate. The financial preparation process will prove tedious in learning and executing, but will enhance your understanding of your business.

15

The Operations Plan

Present Your Objectives and Milestones

Your task in preparing your business plan is to present chosen objectives and milestones that can be used to measure the progress in your company's operations, finance, and marketing. Basically, what benchmarks and progress points tell you and your management team, as well as investors, is that everything is on track, or that something needs attention.

- An *objective* is a clearly defined, achievable timetable, and measurable result toward which you work.
- A *milestone* is an important event along the path of achieving an objective.

The process of preparing your plan creates tasks that need to be accomplished. These tasks—when adjusted for the relationships between resources, people, and finances—lead to organizational planning. That planning results in the creation of management systems for planning, control, and motivation. Tasks to be accomplished include decisions and actions that must be done thoughtfully. Organizational planning assigns responsibility for each of these tasks to specific management divisions or positions. Some tasks are functional tasks which must be performed at a specific time, while others can be done in a routine fashion. In defining the tasks in your operational, financial, and marketing programs, ask:

- What has to be accomplished to make this plan work?
- What critical decisions and actions must be taken to make this a successful company?

You must think through the sequence of events and activities required for each major area of your company. Concentrate on critical tasks, not the routine ones. As an example, payroll is important, but routine. Costs analysis and cash flow forecasts are critical. The following is a generic example of critical tasks by functional areas.

Critical Tasks

MARKETING TASKS
    Contact Customers
    Engage Distributors
    Prepare Advertising
    Process Orders
PRODUCTION TASKS
    Schedule Operations
    Train Workers
    Control Costs
    Ship On Time
FINANCIAL TASKS
    Maintain Records
    Analyze Costs
    Project Cash Flows
    Arrange Bank Loans

Good planning sets reasonably flexible goals for the performance of tasks and responds to changes in the company, its operating environment, and the marketplace.

Task/Time Charts

Your challenge is to present your objectives and milestones in a clearly understandable fashion. Task/time charts can assist you in doing this. The easiest way to initially construct these is to think of the three separate parts:

1. *Objective*: What is the major objective?
2. *Milestone*: What are the milestones along the way to achieving the objective?
3. *Tasks*: What are the individual tasks that need to be accomplished to meet the milestones?

Add a time frame to these and you have a task/time chart.

The following is a very small example. The process is really pretty easy to grasp. The challenge is to think through the process carefully as it applies to your company and individual business situation.

Task/Time Chart for a Business Move
(The objective is to move offices)

Milestones/Tasks	Timetable (In Weeks)					
	1	2	3	4	5	6
Relocate Offices						
Contact real estate agent		X				
View possibilities		X	X			
Negotiate lease			X			
Prepare for move				X	X	
Move						X
Advertising						
Contact agencies	X					
Interview agencies	X	X				
Select agency		X				
Prepare ads			X	X		
Schedule ads				X	X	
Ads appear						X

Time/task charts can be very simple, or they can become very complex, covering extended periods (one year or more). Additionally, you can add to the milestone/task part by designating who (persons, departments, teams, team members) is responsible for implementing, overseeing, and accomplishing the tasks and subsequent milestones.

The Operational Side

This section is primarily oriented toward company facilities, manufacturing capability, equipment, and how they tie into your operational functions. Operation plans disclose all present equipment and facilities capabilities; and your future projections for offices, branches, manufacturing, and distribution. It often helps to include current floor plans and expected future space plans for production or manufacturing companies.

For emerging growth companies, task/time charts can be especially useful in this section. They help impress on the reader that the entrepreneur has a real handle on the operational challenge.

Additionally, you should discuss the day-to-day functions of your company. A lot of it may seem to be boring details, so be careful not to overdo it. This section is your opportunity to impress the reader, or yourself, with your grasp of the fundamentals of operating your business.

Facilities

Your facilities may range from one room in your house, to many locations. Your goal is to develop a word and pictorial understanding of what your present space needs and uses are, then to anticipate short-term and long-term plans.

For Both Product (Manufacturing) and Service Companies

Describe your present or anticipated physical location and size in square feet, its present capacity, why it is appropriate, and its advantageous, or disadvantageous for customers and/or suppliers. Give details where relevant, on the number of floors, type of construction, improvements, lot size, needed improvements, and ownership.

Discuss your location, as applicable, for access to transportation, utilities, and labor. What local taxes, regulations, and zoning restrictions apply to your location?

Discuss personnel, special training, labor supply and availability, skill levels, insurance, and how new technology—including office and virtual technology—affects operations.

If you are currently operating:

- Include the present percent of capacity for your workforce, equipment, and facilities; the excess capacity the company can sell or lease, and how you handle and process customer orders, including a list of who is responsible for what in each process.
- Run a similar list for employee health and safety; customer satisfaction and follow-up; and licenses, permits and regulatory needs, where applicable.

Production Plans

Production planning is about increasing output, reducing costs, and improving quality. It has a place in service and retail companies, as well as large manufacturing concerns. The details of putting together a full manufacturing production plan are best left to other books which cover this important topic in depth.

For Service Firms

Address applicable points above and describe (with drawings if it helps the reader):

- Areas with special uses
- Future expansions
- Full- and part-time labor
- Proximity to customers

For Retail Companies

Describe how the location, product mix, the timing of entry into business, and other specific details that show how the company intends to improve its bottom line.

For Product Manufacturing Companies

If the company is presently involved in manufacturing or assembly operations, cover the following points for your immediate needs projected forward for one to five years. Show how your facilities and processes affect the success and bottom line profit of your company.

- Trace your complete manufacturing process, showing office and work flow layouts from receiving materials through the production stages to finished product storage, giving details on assembly line flows, quality inspections, and other processes.
- Provide information on clean rooms, hazardous materials, environmental and temperature controls, special handling, security, regulated waste disposal, and fire control.
- Describe the items or components handled by outside sources or subcontractors, with details on how these companies can deliver to your specifications.
- Explain special qualities like just-in-time delivery, storage facilities, off-site inventory sites, rolling stock, job-shop versus mass production outfit, the percent of labor in cost of goods, and byproducts.
- Discuss who is responsible for critical steps, product quality tests, employee motivation, and customer satisfaction.
- Describe inventory valuation, management control and tracking systems, shelf lives and turnovers for raw materials and finished goods. How do you compare to industry averages?

Answer these questions:

- What production advantages do you have?
- What is your present capacity? How soon will this need to be expanded?
- Where are your critical parts? Do you have back-up vendors? What are the lead times for these critical components?
- What are the differences for production costs at standard production rates versus different volume levels?

Research and Development (R&D)

Write an R&D section if yours is a product, service, or innovation company. Explain past research and development efforts and accomplishments; discuss future expectations. Justify past time and dollar expenditures. Substantiate proprietary processes, patentable inventions, proprietary processes, or other technology advantages the company will have over its competition and the anticipated market impact of these advantages.

If you did not address the following research and development points while describing your product or service in the business description section, do so here:

- What is your patent, trademark, or copyright position?
- How much is patented, trademarked, or copyrighted?
- How comprehensive and effective are these? According to whom?
- Which companies have technology that is superior to yours?
- Can you make additions to your patents, trademarks, or copyrights to further protect your position? Do you have any further proprietary points or secrecy areas that further enhance your position?
- How do you handle proprietary intellectual property issues?

If you are a retail operation, perhaps you're thinking about adding a new department or changing the focus of a product line. Discuss your line of investigative thinking and support how this action will bring in new customers, enable you to sell more to existing customers, add significant revenues (to offset the additional investment risk), and increase your profits.

In general, discuss your past achievements, present efforts, and future goals; and the risks, strategies, schedules, and expected results from your research and development efforts. All companies, whether product or service, need to have some type of ongoing development. A company that stands still is falling behind.

Early Stage Design and Development

If a major part of, or your whole business plan, is based on the design and development of a new product or service concept, you need to approach the research and development area from a different viewpoint. A great deal of the explanation about your plans will be disclosed under the Product section. Any prospective financing source will have major concerns that will center around the following broad categories:

- *Status of development*. Describe the current status.
- *Remaining tasks*. Describe tasks that need to be accomplished.
- *Outside expertise*. Describe the independent resources obtained.
- *Identify major risks*. What problems are anticipated?
- *Discuss difficulties*. How do they affect timing and costs?
- *Improvements*. What on-going design is needed?
- *Costs*. Present a detailed budget.
- *The "Edge."* Describe what proprietary knowledge or patent you will achieve.

Risks and Problems

These could be a red flag. There are diverse opinions about the inclusion of this category. Some financing sources object to the obvious and prefer to discover their own negatives. Others prefer that the company openly acknowledges risks and potential problems. It's a toss-up, but if you have high-profile, success-threatening risks, you should mention them and note how you will address them. Samples include:

- Fast-changing or fad markets; e.g., children's toys, high fashion.
- A single source of supply.
- Entering a field with large corporate competition.
- If you are a single product or service company.
- Selling to a very small market segment.
- Bringing a new, product or service to market.
- A highly specialized or high technology market.

Legal Issues

If individuals, officers, or your company have past, present, or anticipated litigation or judgments, state this fact. If you have developed operational manuals, for hiring, personnel procedures, purchasing, sales, service, safety, policy, marketing, performance standards, or any other subjects, point this out. Make note of the fact that these are available for review by interested parties.

Summary

The operations side of every business is different. Nonetheless, it still requires the entrepreneurs' attentions when writing their business plans. You should address your facilities' needs, any research and development that you are involved with or contemplate, and the risks and problems, as appropriate. Be brief and draw a succinct picture.

Scheduling, point by point, is an important part of business planning. Many entrepreneurs seldom use scheduling in its various forms. For the Leading Edge planner, it's a necessity. However, if you present your scheduling in graphic form, in a task/time chart, it's easy to initiate, and simpler to follow.

16

Support Documents

As you complete your business plan writing process, consider the back-up and support items to include in the plan or to have available upon request. The type and the number of these can vary considerably.

You do not need to supply these with your business plan unless they are critical to achieving a full understanding of your company. However, you should refer to their availability in the appropriate sections of your plan. Then, in the Appendix, those documents available upon request. Be sure that you do have them, neatly copied and bound, if and when they are requested.

Appendix

The first item in your Appendix should be a glossary (if pertinent), with definitions of *all* technical terms, jargon, and industry "buzz phrases." This is a *must* for technically or scientifically oriented companies.

Additionally, include all essential pieces of evidence, such as resumes, product brochures, customer listings, testimonials, and news articles.

Resumes

Include a resume for each principal and officer. These do not have to be lengthy, in fact, one page resumes are preferable.

Owner's Financial Statement

If your company is a sole proprietorship, a partnership, or a closely held corporation, the financing source will probably request personal financial statements on the principals. Personal tax statements may also be requested. Most lenders have a standard form for you to fill out.

If you have an existing business, most lenders will ask you for, or order on their own accord, a copy of both your personal and company credit reports. If you don't have these, or if it has been some time since you have seen them, it is advisable that you get copies to be sure that the reports are correct. Address this prior to a formal financing request.

Letters of Intent

In the event that you have one or more potential customers who have agreed to buy or represent your product or service, supply copies of their letters of intent. This is also true for a subcontractors, manufacturers, critical suppliers, or other persons or companies with whom you have arranged an association that can lend creditability to your project.

Contracts and Leases

Copies of current contracts are frequently requested. These can include other loans, vehicle purchases, service contracts, purchase agreements on equipment, and any ongoing contracts you may have with suppliers. Also, if you have contracts to furnish products or services to your customers, these can be very valuable to show your existing relationships or substantiate back-orders.

Current lease agreements for buildings, offices, equipment, vehicles, etc., are frequently requested.

Legal Documents

Some financial sources will request copies of your articles of incorporation, bylaws, recent corporate minutes, partnership agreements, property or vehicle titles, copyrights, patents, trademarks, or city or local permits and licenses. It's not unusual to receive requests for insurance agreements as well as for other documents that pertain to the legal aspects of your operations.

In the event that you or your company is involved with patents, trademarks, or copyrights, you should furnish a copy of them in the Appendix. If there are many, you can simply supply a list and refer to the fact that full copies are available upon request.

Reference Letters

These are divided into two categories, business and personal. Business references pertain to those written by customers, suppliers, associates, and various trade organizations to which you may belong.

Personal references are usually not provided unless requested. These are furnished by both business and nonbusiness associates who can affirm and attest to your business skills and personal or community standing.

Miscellaneous

There are numerous other documents that you may have referred to throughout your plan. These may include demographic studies, marketing reports, maps, procedure manuals for personnel and policy, technical or scientific reports and papers, competitive information, specialized studies, newspaper or magazine articles, bibliographies, reference sources, trade association studies, and other support documents. Consider carefully which are important for inclusion in your Appendix and which should be available by request.

*E*pilogue

A Final Thought on Planning

A survey that we participated in of more than 1,000 successful entrepreneurial companies showed some interesting facts. Of the respondents, 89 percent indicated that their plan is always used to set goals for employees and to establish rewards for management. For these entrepreneurs, the top three reasons for keeping a plan up-to-date were: (1) accessing customer needs, (2) competitive analysis, and (3) the continuing analysis of the economics of delivering products and services. Forty-five percent of the companies updated their plans for two- to five-year periods, 44 percent updated for two years at a time; 29 percent updated annually, and 39 percent updated quarterly.

As to hitting their goals, 45 percent reported only a slight year-end variance in goal achievement. Interestingly, the longer-term planners who up-dated quarterly were the most successful in obtaining their goals. Finally, one of the top success approaches seems to come from establishing goals that take at least a full-quarter to implement. This reinforces our contention that *good planning is a detailed, complex, and ongoing process.*

Planning—Why Do It?

- Charts a clear direction
- Ensures consistent decision making
- Helps management allocate resources most effectively
- Builds commitment and orientation to a common purpose
- Anticipates problems and creates methods of dealing with them
- Establishes a basis for evaluating company and individual performance

- Provides a framework for facilitating a quick response to changed conditions
- Defines in measurable and objective terms what is most important and what needs to be achieved

What Professional Investors Look For

Because of the high volume of plans they see each year (compared to the number of deals they complete), the first thing professional investors seek is something in the plan that lets them say no quickly. They are also experts at determining how serious the plan writers are and they rely on the executive summary to clearly show the nature of the project, the amount of money needed, sales and earning forecasts, and the makeup of the management team. It's like the first 30 seconds of eye contact in a romantic encounter: If a quick scan doesn't cut it, you won't get the opportunity to make the pitch.

What Every Money Source Asks

If your plan doesn't address the following points, you won't get funded until you can provide the answers. *Do it right the first time!*

- *How much money do you need and in what stages?* Be specific. If you can't state a figure, you're not prepared to ask.
- *What do you plan to use the money for?* Your answer reveals your money priorities.
- *How will the money improve your business?* If you can't show how every dollar will make more dollars in return, you won't get serious investor attention.
- *How are you going to pay the money back?* Naturally this is a biggie to a lender, and an equity investor wants to know when, how, and how much they're going to get out.
- *What's "Plan B"?* If your first plan doesn't work out, what alternates are you putting into place.

Entrepreneurial Plans Take Your Best Effort

All companies should have a business plan. However, if a company's objective is to be a high growth, Leading Edge company, it *must* have a business plan, and that plan must be detailed and flexible. Preparing it may take months, but you won't get to first base without it. The outlines presented in this book may not fit every company's particular requirements exactly, but should contain enough general information and suggestions to provide a solid base for preparing your plan.

The primary reason for solid business planning is to put your company at a competitive advantage in the future. You know where you stand today; secure your place in your market for tomorrow. Keep in mind that planning is a process rather than a goal. While implementing the planning process, you will discover things not only about your market, your company, and your customers, but also about yourself.

Failing to plan is planning to fail.
● ● ● ● ●

A company should give its plan its very best efforts. You will discover that a well-prepared Leading Edge plan will prove a solid sales tool when approaching any financing source—investor or lender. It also will provide management with a written game plan for guiding operations and maintaining a check on expectations.

Additional information and updates to this book can be found on the Web at: www.venturea.com.

Appendix

Summary Business Plans

Feasibility Study for Online Mapping Service

Executive Summary

Introduction

Online Mapping Service (OMS) will distribute and sell maps over the Internet. Internet distribution permits three major innovations, at lower prices, than existing map outlets:

1. Just-in-time delivery (JIT)
2. Digitized, cross-referenced map features and options can be customized by the customer. Information from different maps can be compiled into one.
3. The customer can add, view, change, or eliminate details before the purchase.

OMS will start operations from a home office, on a small scale, with variations on one product—geological survey maps for hikers. Geological survey map features include:

- Area boundaries, size, scale, features, and other layout items as determined by customer.
- Global positioning satellite (GPS) grid points can be laid onto contour maps so that walkers and explorers can accurately pinpoint their position, and so never get lost.
- Roads, structures, and other designations can be placed onto the map.

These features, and others, come from information scanned by the Company from maps or loaded from CDs. After distribution, the customer can print paper maps for field use. If this concept is successful, the Company will add product lines, based on different markets for maps and mapping, in successive years. Some projected markets include:

- Map packages covering entire trail systems for specific end users, such as the Boy Scouts.
- Exploration site maps. Geological survey maps, marketed with specific features to selected industrial, commercial, and governmental users.
- Geological Survey maps of other countries as they become available on CDs.

- Genetic, biology, biotechnology, chemistry, and other science maps, overlays, and charts.

The Company has another potential revenue stream available through licensing its

- distribution model to existing map stores and recreational and business outlets.
- proprietary software to other Web commerce firms wishing to enable, "Try it before you buy it" solutions.

Purpose

This study was written to estimate the business potential for the Company to profitably enter the map business on the Internet. To minimize costs, only one product line—geological contour maps of the United States, with various options—forms the basis of the tests.

The Company competes with existing map outlets, both on and off the Internet. The purpose of the study is to see if this type of mapping company can reach the point of profitably in its first year on the World Wide Web with one product line.

The study will focus on market demand, potential, size, and resulting revenues. Assumptions will be checked against a pro forma revenue model for one year. The results determine if the owner stays or leaves his present job to devote his full-time services to the Company. A second purpose is to determine whether a Company based solely on a personal investment can profitably compete in its market segments.

Preliminary Assumptions

The Company assumes

- there is sufficient market potential to warrant a new retail entry on the Internet.
- the demand for maps will increase as the technology to create them, and the number of people using the Internet, goes up.
- the Company can generate adequate income in its trial map areas.
- the Company can develop and maintain sufficient technical expertise to compete in a rapidly changing technology, commerce, and regulatory environment.
- the Company can obtain the necessary copyrights and other map information to maintain a commercial advantage.

- it is possible for the Company to commence operations with one employee—the owner—and little, or no, outside investment.

Market Potential

Environmental Analysis

The Internet is rapidly growing in the U.S. and abroad. In 1998 electronic commerce on the Internet was estimated between $4–7 billion by various firms. This amount is increasing at an annual rate more than 300 percent.

Trade journals that measure connections and traffic on the Web show it currently receives 55 million visitors who come at least once per week. Industry, retail, and merchant industry sources claim that between 25 percent and 54 percent of Internet visitors go shopping—or make purchase decisions—online.

Estimates of visitor traffic show it as growing at a rate approaching 40 percent per month. The recent adoption of SET (Secure Electronic Transaction) protocols has been projected to double the rate of commercial entries. Assuming a 1998 Internet e-commerce market size of $5.5 billion, at a growth rate of 500 percent, the market will pass $137 billion by the year 2000.

A search for Internet-based map companies found millions of listings. All relevant listings among the first 300 sites offered U.S. city street maps with directions to find address locations. One major software firm had announced a joint program with the U.S. Geological Survey to distribute contour maps on the Web, but to date this site does not appear to exist.

Only four sites offered some form of geological survey maps. These other entries do not offer the sizing, customization, or payment features of the Company.

More exploration maps are sold in the world today than ever before. In the U.S. five factors lead to increased numbers of potential customers: (1) an increasing population, (2) environmental awareness, (3) the addition of wilderness areas, (4) a growing appetite for the outdoors, and (5) a continuing trend towards outdoor activities.

The concept of additional features has been demonstrated as valid by the proliferation of geographic information system (GIS) companies. An industry barely ten years old, last year GIS firms in the U.S. are estimated to have sold more than $10 billion of information.

Strengths

- The owner has used U.S. Geological Survey, and similar maps, in the western United States for 20 years. He understands contour maps, their uses, and can see how electronic customization can improve their value and use by others. He is experienced with the Internet, has developed Web sites and understands the nature of electronic commerce. His technical background is sufficient to oversee the development of proprietary software.
- Most of the technology underlying the Company's software is already in existence and freely available. CD maps of the U.S., most of Europe, the mid-East, parts of Africa, and the oceans are available in digitized formats. The recent development of high speed asynchronous digital line technology (ASDL), combined with SET protocols makes it possible to transfer a huge amount of information over telephone lines at a low cost for the technology.
- Another strength is the Company's recognition of *which* technology changes were needed to improve customer trust and retain a positive image with early buyers, while still offering commerce operations that match the Internet's desired model of fast, easy, powerful, and inexpensive service. Concentrating technology efforts on proprietary software that lets people create and view the finished map on the Internet, *before making payment*, brings a convenience and trust level that distinguishes this Company from its competitors.
- Because the Company operates entirely online, the only overhead costs are for software development, copyrights, licenses, and the time/labor to scan images.

Weaknesses

- This Company will be brand new. The owner has no prior experience or demonstrated competence in the core business areas: maps, distribution, or retail sales.

  As a child the owner worked for several years in his family's retail business. He understands the importance of servicing the customers needs. His Web development experience taught him the value of keeping technology simple, preferably out of sight of the customer.
- Other companies with better financing, more experience, and greater resources than the Company, are certain to enter this market, if they have not already done so.

  The proprietary technology, and the recognition for its need, makes barriers for competitors very high unless or until they develop similar technology and service arrangements. This is expected to take 6 to 12 months for competitors with deep pockets—from the time they recognize the problem. The Company plans to continue to exploit any technology lead.

- The Internet is an unknown to most people, particularly those over the age of 50. If its technology does not become easier, or if the actual process to download the maps takes too long, then people will not use the service.

  The Internet's growth is already so large and fast that even if the market slows dramatically from its current rate, it will still offer many competitive advantages to the currently existing outlet base.

- Sales and revenues are based on estimates for Internet visitor traffic and growth rates. These numbers vary wildly from company to company.

  The Company assumed a very conservative 10 percent return rate on these numbers. It then decided to adopt a figure 7.5 percent lower, based on the more conservative formula-driven sales estimate.

Costs

The success of the Online Mapping Service depends on the benefit/cost relationship. The following section deals with direct start-up costs. Incremental costs will be assessed with little attempt to allocate overhead costs in this section.

Start-up costs have been broken into two groups, (1) product development costs and (2) company start-up costs:

Product Development Costs

U.S. Geological Survey CD Mapping Service	$ 2,856 for U.S. mountain states
Licensing fees for other mapping services	$ 8,000 (estimated)
Licensing attorney	$ 3,500
Global Positioning Satellite (GPS) software	$ 595 to insert grids
Global Positioning scanner	$ 459 for testing purposes
Optical Character Recognition (OCR) software	$ 550 to read map CDs
Top of the line scanner	$ 1,700
Computer Aided Design (CAD) software	$ 600
Adobe Photoshop™ (graphics) software	$ 579
Other scanning software	$ 575
Software training	$ 600 (estimated)
Contract labor to scan maps for two months	$ 5,800 (estimated)

Testing maps (by driving in state)	$ 200 (1 week) gas, food, telephone
Other travel, airfare, hotel, meals	$ 1,800 (estimated)
Long distance telephone calls	$ 200
Subtotal	$28,014
Other product expenses @ 10%	$ 2,801
Subtotal	$30,815

Company Start-Up Costs

Personal salary	$ 3,000 for one month
Computer server lease deposit	$ 400
Outside software programmers	$ 4,800
Domain names registration	$ 140 for two Web addresses
Phone lease deposit	$ 400 for T-1 lines
Supplies	$ 200
Internet advertising	$ 3,000
Legal fees	$ 500 for incorporation
Technical writer	$ 3,500
Web site development	$ 3,000
Printed materials/brochures	$ 850
Graphics	$ 1,200
Insurance	$ 275
Other	$ 650
	$21,915

Monthly Expenses

Sales and Marketing Expenses (Monthly)

Internet publicity/advertising	$ 1,400
PR Newswire™/other services	$ 550
Print/other advertising	$ 2,000
Press releases/other writing	$ 800
	$ 4,750
Other Expenses @ 10%	$ 475
	$ 5,225

Salaries + Personnel Costs (Monthly)

Personal salary	$ 3,000
Benefits @ 35%	$ 1,050
Other/contract labor	$ 1,500
	$ 5,550

General and Administrative Expenses (Monthly)

Computer server lease	$	400 includes firewall/secure commerce
Utilities	$	80
Insurance	$	75
Liability insurance	$	65 in case people get lost and sue
High speed telephone access	$	126
Additional programming	$	400/month (estimated)
Accounting/tax service	$	900
Printing	$	125
Postage/shipping	$	85
Bank account	$	45
Other supplies	$	150
	$	2,451
Other (contingent @ 10%)	$	245
	$	2,696

Based on the primary costs the Company foresees an annual cost to operate in the personal mapping market of approximately:

One-Time Costs

Start-up	$21,915
Product start-up	30,815
Product expense (annual)	15,229
	$67,959

Monthly Costs

Sales & Marketing	$ 5,225
Salaries	5,550
General & Administrative	2,696
	$13,471/month × 11 months in first year = $148,181

Total 1st Year Expenses = $67,959 + $148,181 = $216,140

Cost Assumptions

- The Company obtained preliminary cost estimates from five map vendors. Preliminary estimates from three of these companies were extrapolated to estimate the costs for all five. In the process, two other potential map sources were found.
- The Company can purchase CDs of the U.S. Geological Survey maps, plus other information not generally known to the public, for the price shown.
- The cost to develop a proprietary advance view software, with built-in antitheft protection was twice the programmer's estimate.
- Prices for software, scanners, and other equipment generally were reached by estimating 35 percent over the prices shown in ads by a local retail outlet to acquire higher end, longer lasting equipment. All equipment prices were shown as purchases (versus renting or leasing).

Revenues, Expenses, and Benefits

Objectives.

- Establish a presence on the Internet and sell maps starting in the first month of operations. (*Note*: The Company does not consider contract programmer's time, or its owner's R&D, as a business month.)
- Publicize the hiking map Web site to 1,500 potential customers online, and to 50–100 trade and consumer journals and newspapers in the first month.
- Reach a sales goal averaging 5,000 maps per month, at $7 each (assuming a map price inflation rate of 5 percent per year), starting in the third month.
- Sell 43,500 maps (0.001 percent of last year's market, assuming no growth) by the end of the 12th month.
- Repay entire investment costs within first year of operations.
- Acquire sufficient capital through in-house sales to expand operations into other areas at an assumed cost of $25,000 per product/ market area of expansion.

Revenues

Revenues are determined by defining the Market Segments of potential customers, followed by four steps:

1. Establishing the potential market demand from these customers
2. Establishing the potential market size based on the demand from these customers
3. Determining a factor showing the degree of market availability by the Company.
4. Forecasting sales based on the idea of substituting a superior product, with added features, at no extra cost and greater convenience to the customer.

Market segments.

The Company sells maps entirely online. Its buyer is a person who goes to the mountains for pleasure or business.

- Pleasure walkers include hikers, skiers, backpackers, bicyclers, 4-wheelers, hunters, fishers, picnickers, and other tourists or sporting enthusiasts.
- Business customers include exploration, mining, land development, information, engineering, construction, highway and other types of firms; state and federal land and resource agencies, private institutions, universities, associations, groups, clubs, and others.

Potential Market Demand.

The potential market demand equals the total number of similar maps sold in one year, for which this Company's product can be substituted. The owner decided the most accurate measure of demand was actual sales. He estimated that 37 million maps, of a nature similar to those of the Company, were sold in the U.S. in the last year. These sales volume estimates came from four sources:

1. 12 USGS maps sold in 1997 (Supt. of Documents, U.S. Government Printing Office)
2. 12 million maps from other companies (industry statistics nearly match government figures).
3. 6 million outdoor club members (estimated to buy two maps per year per member)
4. 1 million global positioning satellite (GPS) monitors (associated with three map sales each)

= 31 million maps—the potential market demand

Potential Market Size.

Potential market size = number of maps sold × the
average sale price per map

= 31,000,000 maps × $6.85/map
= $253, 450,000—the potential market size for hiking maps in the U.S.
per year.

Market Availability Factor.

Through statistics from the U.S. Census Bureau, Internet, and computer trade magazines, the Company developed information that showed potential segments of the overall market:

- 14.8% of the U.S. population lives in mountain states.
- × 20.3% of the U.S. population has regular Internet access.
- × 20.0% of all printers sold in have sufficient resolution to print high quality maps.
- × 80.0% of all people in the U.S. are between 13 and 55, the most likely age for map users.

= .148 × .203 × .20 × .80
= .004807—Market availability factor. Based on this factor the Company will attempt to sell (reach) one-half of 1 percent of the total map market.

Sales Forecast.

Sales were estimated in two ways:

1. Sales = the Market availability factor x total market size x market penetration by Company
   = .004807 × $253,000 × .25 (estimated at reaching one person in four)
   = $304,583
2. Gross pro forma sales = $367,592 (on the spreadsheet)
   Net pro forma sales = $321,643

The Company chose to use sales amount reached by formula, $304,583, a lower number as potentially more accurate.

Revenue Forecast.

Annual net revenues were derived by estimating monthly expenses, adding these expenses to the start-up costs, and carrying the total through one year.

Net revenues equal the gross revenues – Expenses.

Gross revenues	$304,583
– Expenses	–216,140
= Net revenues of	$ 88,443

Revenue Assumptions

1. The company's pro forma statement for this feasibility study did not take financing charges or taxes into account.
2. It estimated some expenses and assumed percentages of annual sales as costs for other expense items.
3. The Company added 10 percent to each expense category.
4. Assuming an overestimation of revenues by formula, the Company revised its Annual Revenues downward by an additional 25 percent.

Gross revenues	$304,583 × 0.75 = $228,437
– Expenses	–216,140
= Net revenues of	$ 12,297

5. Industry figures, or estimates based on industry statistics, are used throughout the model.
6. USGS retail map price of $4.75 came from the lowest price given by store managers for a nationwide chain of outdoor recreation equipment companies.
7. Other maps were priced around $8.95 each, based on owner's personal survey.
8. Other map sales, overall, were assumed to equal those of the USGS, based on conversations with map store owners and managers.
9. The average map price was used as the map sale price.

Return on Investment (ROI)

$$\text{Return on Investment (ROI)} = \frac{\text{Net Profit}}{\text{Total Investment}}$$

To start, the owner needs $70,000. Because this is the bare minimum to cover his risk, he adds $5,000 as a reserve for a total of $75,000.

Net Profit = Gross Revenues – Expenses

= 1.18 × initial investment = 118% in the first year.

Based on its initial revenue $\dfrac{\$(304{,}583 - 216{,}140)}{\$75{,}000} = \dfrac{\$88{,}443}{\$75{,}000}$
projections ROI =

If the owner assumes online returns 25 percent less than its projected $304,000, which is certainly reasonable, then:

$$\text{Return on Investment (ROI)} = \frac{\text{Net Profit}}{\text{Total Investment}}$$

$$\text{ROI} = \frac{\$228{,}437}{\$75{,}000} = \frac{\$12{,}297}{\$75{,}000}$$

= 0.163 x initial investment or 16.3% in the first year.

Conclusions and Recommendations

The concept merits the attempt. The Company can self-fund its first-year growth, based solely on the estimated number of visitors and subsequent sales percentage numbers.

The high start-up costs (estimated at $75,000), can be lowered by 20–30 percent if the owner slashes all costs, including his salary, to the bone. Still, this high up-front cost leads to the conclusion that some outside form of investment or debt capital is necessary to start the business.

Should the Company's sales efforts fail, its technology may hold sufficient value to return all early investment costs.

Recommendations

- The owner cuts all possible costs.
- The Company is dependent on Internet-driven visitor traffic. It must do everything in its power to bring in visitors, satisfy them, and get them to return to buy again. One way to do this is to develop the software technology, then immediately look to strategic alliance, or licensing, to gain either brand recognition or visitor traffic through another domain.
- At $60/hour his initial programming cost is $4,800. He can personally invest this amount of money, just to see if it is possible to acquire his proprietary development.

Information Used

- U.S. population: 270,000,000
- U.S. mountain state population: 40,000,000
- U.S. Internet (Web) users: 55,000,000
- High resolution (600 dpi) laser and deskjet printer sales: 11,000,000.
- U.S. Geological Survey map sales: 12,500,000/year.
- Others geological terrain and contour maps sold, assumed to equal 12,500,000.
- Global positioning satellite monitor sales exceeded 250,000 per year for seven years. Figures for four years used in this estimate. Three contour maps are assumed for every GPS monitor.
- Outdoor recreation, nature, hiking, hunting, bicycling and other group memberships totaled more than eight million. Six million were assumed for estimate. Each member is assumed to buy two contour maps per year.

Appendix

- Specifications for software development.
- Agreement with software designer.

Reader Note: To verify the revenue projections used in the study, the owner created a revenue estimate for first-year revenues. These revenue estimates showed higher revenues than were determined by formula. The owner chose to use the lower revenue figures from the formula-based revenue projections. The revenue estimate spreadsheet is shown below.

Online Mapping Service
Feasibility Study Pro Forma Sales Estimate Year 1

Unit Sales per Month	1	2	3	4	5	6	7	8	9	10	11	12	Annual
Press release, e-mail, etc.													
Web directory/ search/ISPs	275	385	539	755	1,056	1,479	2,071	2,899	4,058	5,682	7,955	11,136	38,290
Internet newsgroups	3	3	4	5	6	8	10	12	15	19	23	29	136
E-mail	60	84	118	165	230	323	452	632	885	1,240	1,736	2,430	1,398
PR Newswire	25	26	28	29	30	32	34	35	37	39	41	43	398
Other business PR firms	50	53	55	58	61	64	67	70	74	78	81	86	796
Outdoor companies	6	5	6	6	6	6	7	7	7	8	8	9	81
Selected corporate executives	40	42	44	46	49	51	54	56	59	62	65	68	637
Club, associations, groups	125	131	138	145	152	160	168	176	185	194	204	214	1,990
Subtotal sales	584	729	931	1,208	1,591	2,122	2,860	3,888	5,321	7,320	10,112	14,014	50,680
Repeat/referral	–	29	36	47	60	80	106	143	194	266	366	506	1,833
Total Unit Sales	584	759	967	1,254	1,651	2,202	2,966	4,031	5,515	7,586	10,478	14,520	52,513
Total Unit Sales @ $7 ea.	$4,085	$5,310	$6,770	$8,780	$11,559	$15,411	$20,764	$28,217	$38,606	$53,103	$73,349	$101,639	$367,592
Minus credit charges @ 3.5%	$ 143	$ 186	$ 237	$ 307	$ 405	$ 539	$ 727	$ 988	$ 1,351	$ 1,859	$ 2,567	$ 3,557	$ 12,866
Minus e-shrinkage @ 10%	$ 408	$ 531	$ 677	$ 878	$ 1,156	$ 1,541	$ 2,076	$ 2,822	$ 3,861	$ 5,310	$ 7,335	$ 10,164	$ 36,759
Total Adjustments	$ 551	$ 717	$ 914	$1,185	$ 1,561	$ 2,080	$ 2,803	$ 3,810	$ 5,212	$ 7,169	$ 9,902	$ 13,731	$ 49,626
Adjusted Gross Revenues	$3,534	$4,593	$5,856	$7,595	$ 9,998	$13,331	$17,961	$24,407	$33,394	$45,934	$63,447	$ 87,918	$317,967

Assumptions

1. 55,000,000 people visit the Internet per month.
2. 0.0001% (1/10,000) of 55,000,000 Web viewers visit site.
3. Newsgroups and e-mail send 0.0001% (1/10,000) of visitors to site.
4. Web growth rate of 40% per month.
5. Newsgroup growth rate of 25% per month.
6. E-mail visitor growth rate at 40% per month.
7. Visitor numbers from business, club sources, are estimated based on opinions of salespeople.
8. 5% of site visitors buy a map at some point during the month.
9. Visitor numbers increase, matching assumed Internet growth rate of 40% (actual figure is 60%).
10. Referral/repeats from purchasers grow at 5% per month, (adjusted down for seasonal changes).
11. Maps sold at $7 each
12. Taxes not shown.
13. Numbers vary due to formula rounding.

Luminous Paint Products, Inc.

1. Executive Summary

Luminous Paint Products, Inc., manufactures and distributes innovative, specialty paint coatings and fiberglass repair paste for use on spas, boats, swimming pools, and in other harsh environments. Its home office is in St. Louis, Missouri.

Products are sold by the owner, in the Midwest and several other states. The Company will be self-funded, with expansion limited by manufacturing and inventory considerations and costs. Growth is expected with continued successful applications over time and subsequent industry recognition. Company objectives include additional distribution to new areas and/or customer types on 6–9 month basis.

The Company is self-funded, using advance payment for current jobs as seed capital for operations. In its first year, Luminous Paint Products, Inc., projects a $65,000 profit. The owner has invested an additional $10,000 to cover losses and reserves.

Objectives

1. To gain and maintain a steady sales volume in excess of $20,000/month, in the first year.
2. To pass all industry tests for steel surfaces in marine and harsh environments.
3. To acquire manufacturer's representatives and achieve national distribution after passing industry tests.
4. To create and develop a market for sales in fiberglass repair.
5. To manufacture in-house by the second quarter of year two.
6. To add sales, marketing, and administrative personnel before the second year.
7. To gain a foothold (5 percent or more) of the marine steel paint and coating industry within five years.
8. To sell the Company, or license its formulas, to another firm in three years.

2. The Company

Luminous Paint Products, Inc., manufactures and distributes an innovative series of specialty coatings from a rented 500-square-foot office in St. Louis, Missouri. Burmese Production Company of East St. Louis, Illinois, holds a contract to blend products for the company. A 1,000-square-foot warehouse space in the same complex as Burmese has been leased to hold raw materials and finished product.

The original area of operations covers five states near Missouri, test applications in Florida, and two oil refinery and storage projects underway in Wyoming. Based on the success of its initial contracts and research tests, the Company will expand operations into most of its target industries in the U.S. within two years.

Ownership

The Company is privately-held, operated as a Subchapter S Corporation, incorporated in Delaware in 1999. Depending on the circumstances, Luminous Paint Products, Inc., may become a C Corporation, form an alliance or become a strategic partner to a major player, license its formulations, or be acquired by an outside firm.

History

Luminous Paint Products, Inc., resulted from a personal effort by its founder, Ed Dougheny, to fix cracks in his home's fiberglass spa. Available products could not repair the spa, so Ed attempted to create one that did.

He succeeded after three years of spare-time work, and an investment of $4,000 in chemicals, equipment, tools, and materials. After tests showed his paste sealed cracks and holes better than comparable products,

Ed thinned the paste to create a paint. For two years he applied his "paint" to fiberglass boat hulls, concrete swimming pools, steel storage tanks, and every other surface he could find.

The material seemed to work on everything, so Ed looked for a company to manufacture his paint version. He found Burmese Production Company, who agreed to run smaller production batches for his paint line. Ed then sold four jobs to raise enough capital for production batches on paint and primer.

At this point he has decided to sell only from inventory and to leverage the blending firm's expertise, technology, and facilities. Since industry tests are required to enter larger markets, the company has various laboratory and field tests underway. Results are expected during the first year. If these results are favorable, the Company will increase its sales efforts. Until such time, first year sales efforts are limited to Ed's personal capacity to sell product.

Assets

At startup:

Item	Value
40 gallons of paint and primer	$ 800
Personal computer, printer, modem, and software	1,400
The owner's personal car	3,500
(3) Proprietary formulations	60,000
(4) existing contracts	26,100
Tools, jigs, lab and shop equipment	4,000
Existing chemicals/materials supplies	3,200
Total Assets	$99,000

3. Products

Luminous Pool&Spa Paint™ (LPS) is for application to fiberglass, concrete and steel surfaces. Works with or without primer. With primer covers 400 sq. ft./gal.; without 200 sq. ft./gal. Clear/White/Blue. Wholesale $18.00. Retail $27.00.

Luminous Pool&Spa Paint Primerc (LPSP), improves spread and adhesion. Shipped in 1 gal. and 5 gal. sizes. Covers 400 sq. ft./gal. Per gallon: Wholesale $14.00. Retail $25.00

Fiberglass Repair Paste™ (FRP) is LPS concentrated 3X. Paste can be applied directly to dry, wet, or underwater to concrete and fiberglass. White/Blue. Wholesale $17.00/quart.

Fiberglass Repair kits (FRPR) contain: (1) pint of FRP, 4 sq. ft. of fiberglass mesh, three dye colors, and instructions. Wholesale $17.00. Suggested retail $29.95.

Important Features

1. Repairs look better, matching backgrounds more closely than conventional fiberglass.
2. Surface preparation avoids complicated and costly steps.
3. LPS applications wear better than their competitors.

Research/Future Developments

LPS and FRP applications tested on spas, boat hulls, oil storage tanks, and concrete swimming pools. All fiberglass repairs are intact since application, up to three years ago. An inspection for flaws in the applied surfaces, plus microscopic examinations by industry specialists, plus a series of chemical tests by outside laboratories, found no significant signs of wear in time periods up to 18 months—twice that of competitors.

A private lab is testing Luminous products to measure and characterize the properties of LPS and LPS Primer, using known standards. Industry approval is expected in 9–12 months. U.S. Navy and Department of Transportation tests on steel beams look promising after seven months.

A municipal swimming pool in St. Louis shows minimal signs of wear or discoloration after two years of use. Rusty oil storage and separation tanks have not leaked and show no signs of flaws, cracks, or surface degradation after nine months.

Formula Security

The Company protects its formulas with

- an established, written chain of custody.
- signed nondisclosures.
- the use of meaningless chemicals and unneeded procedures in field tests.
- holding the formulas in a safety deposit box.
- other security methods, not mentioned here.

No patents were taken.

Product Inventory

As a first year policy, the Company will not run a commercial batch of LPS or Primer until it receives an order, or group of orders, whose payments ensure batches run at an immediate profit. Paste and kits are limited to the materials in stock, perhaps 50 pints in all.

4. Industry

In the U.S., industrial fiberglass and specialty coatings applications cost $200 billion per year, with material wholesale costs of $22–35 billion. Several companies dominate the industry.

Harsh-environment paints are similar in nature and quality, requiring reapplication in short periods of time, some in as little as one year. Products are either sold as paints or as specialty coatings.

Due to a history of low quality and indifferent application, industrial paints compete on price, with little to distinguish between them. Most profits come from feedstock chemicals. "Paint cookbook" formulations are freely available.

Specialty coatings compete on durability and ease of application over price. Few specialty coatings remain for more than two years.

Margins run higher on coating application than on paint applications. Contractors typically stick with known product lines. Selections are based on regional availability and past reputation.

No clear leader exists within the industry, although a limited range of known products may be specified on most large job bids. Every leading specialty coating industry, except one, is a division or spin-off from one of the big five paint manufacturers.

Success Factors

Specialty coatings are sold to smaller industry niches, usually involving special application requirements such as harsh or corrosive environments; clean surfaces for the medical, food, and computer industries; or special application attributes such as highly corrosive, underwater, or surfaces that are difficult to reach or undergo motion, flexing, pressure, and temperature or other changes.

The industry desires superior performance and wear characteristics; consistent results; acceptable pricing; and reasonable availability. Entry barriers come from contractor and distributor unwillingness to carry unproven or unknown regional products. Resistance to new products is high.

Other success factors include:

- Fewer application steps
- Easier application and cleanup
- Longer lasting, better looking results
- Passing industry mandated tests, or demonstrations to prove superior wear and durability features

Contractors take large risks with new coating. The Company must complete its tests with passing marks to obtain product liability insurance, necessary to sell to the industry.

Chief Competitors

Several companies operate in the specialty coatings industry. Most of these firms are divisions of large chemical companies, or paint industry manufacturers. Due to the high cost of shipping and the differing nature of wear and corrosion, competition is regional in nature; a top product line in one area is seldom the first product in use elsewhere.

The fiberglass industry still uses a multistep process to manufacture products. The Company's repair process competes with methods that differ minimally from the manufacturing process over the past three decades. The opportunity and barriers are high in this industry.

In both areas, the Company expects its superior product results, its lower costs, and easier application processes to bring recognition. Normally both industries sell via stores and distributors. To gain recognition and compete, the Company will sell direct to the source in its first year.

Industry Distribution Methods

Municipal concrete swimming pools must be repainted every 12 to 18 months. No standards for durability exist in the industry. Swimming pool paint is stocked and sold by pool supply distributors. Due to the short duration of these coatings, and the need for continual reapplication on larger sites, job contracts are often set years in advance.

Spas are colored during the manufacturing process. No aftermarket exists to repair older spas, which are replaced when damaged. The Company will approach spa equipment repair suppliers to see if they will stock its products.

Boat and fiberglass swimming pool repairs involve several steps, normally made by pool and boat contractors. For the most part, home repairs have been attempted using fiberglass kits and materials stocked by marine distributors.

Industrial steel paint jobs are serviced by private contractors, who usually specialize by industry and type of surface; e.g., steel structures in marine environments. New paint systems are often presented and sold directly to contractors at trade shows and in classes.

Regulatory Factors

Swimming pool, spa, and steel marine applications involve strong solvents as their base. When applied, these chemicals emit noxious—potentially lethal—fumes. The industry is closely regulated by the various air quality control commissions, the Environmental Protection Agency, and the National Institute of Occupational Safety and Health (NIOSH). Municipal and commercial applications on larger sites require a permit. Shipping must take place in U.S. Department of Transportation–approved containers, with labeling requirement.

Industry Cost Factors

Industry suppliers, distributors and contractors claim it costs $1 million, or more to paint an oil refinery or bridge. One job can run the year around. Material costs are estimated at up to 25 percent of total charges. Shipping charges are an important expense item, limiting distribution to local formulators.

The Company estimates it products will save 40 percent of total job time and 50 percent of labor costs associated with preparation. This will offset the estimated 10–15 percent higher cost per gallon of LPS. The ability to wear longer is an added bonus.

5. Market

Size and Demand

According to industry sources, 112.9 million gallons of specialty coatings were applied to industrial fiberglass, steel, and concrete surfaces in 1997. The wholesale price for these chemicals and coatings were estimated at just under $500 million dollars, exclusive of shipping, application, and other related processes.

The U.S. fiberglass boat market used $130 million dollars worth of surface coating inventory in 1996. Painting and repair prices, primarily for pleasure boats, ran an estimated $80 million plus.

Every year two million spa units are sold in the U.S. The typical spa runs for three years before it needs extensive repairs. Most units are replaced 5–6 years after installation. An estimated two million units require repairs each year, with repair estimates at $800 per unit.

In October, 1998, *Swimming Pool Magazine*, showed that municipal concrete swimming pools are resurfaced every 21 months. Paint and materials costs total $18,600 on average, with down time in excess of one month. Some 200,000 pools are repainted each year in the U.S.

Target Markets

The Company sells products directly to contractors or to supply companies under contract to large painting and repair firms. All year one and two markets are regional in nature, confined to within 400 miles of the factory to save shipping costs. Year one and year two markets primarily include:

- Painting concrete pools
- Painting industrial steel tanks in oil production fields
- Repairs to fiberglass spas and boats.

Based on its developments and test outcomes, Luminous Paint Products expects to enter the marine market for steel and concrete surface applications in the second quarter of its second year.

Customer Loyalty and Attitudes

Surveys show strong specialty coatings brand loyalty by industrial contractors. Unlike the close ties between manufacturer and outlets in the paint industry, coating lines turn over on a regular basis. In the Company's opinion, much of the swimming pool, fiberglass, and steel market are still open to products demonstrated to perform better than current products used.

Pricing and Payment Strategy

The Company's products wholesale at 10–15 percent over typical competitor paints. To gain market entry, the Company offers a 10 percent discount for advance payment on its LPS and LPS Primer line. The Company believes its superior application and wear qualities, combined with a discount, will offset its higher price.

Distribution Strategy

The Company intends to offer just-in-time delivery. All quoted prices are FOB. The manufacturer agrees to run minimum batches of 200 gallons or more within ten business days of receiving the order.

Once an application has been shown to work within a particular industry sector, the Company will then obtain distributors from known suppliers to that sector. As part of the process to obtain these distributors, the Company will enter into coop advertising and other publicity programs, including direct demonstrations at trade shows.

Sales Strategy

The Company owner will sell its LPS line directly

- to industrial paint contractors, with an emphasis on gaining access to approved vendor lists.
- by direct project bids, undertaken through subcontractors to the Company.
- to boat building, marina, and spa stores and supply distributors.
- to cities and pool installers and other firms that build, own, or repair large swimming pools.

Promotion

The Company will promote its products via

- cooperative trade show booths.
- articles, press releases, and new product announcements to trade journals.
- direct sales calls on facilities' operators and industrial paint contractors.

6. Operations

License to Manufacture

The Burmese Manufacturing Company, a custom paint manufacturer in East St. Louis, Illinois, will make 200-, 500-, or 1,000-gallon batches of LPS or LPS Primer. This custom blender has been in business for 28 years. It has mixing contracts with several state highway departments and several large industrial concerns who used products similar to the Company's line. The owner has met with the Burmese CEO and has a reasonable familiarity and rapport with their operation.

Operating in two shifts, 38 management and line employees produce various coatings and paints for some 25 different companies and distributors. The Company maintains a chemist on staff to ensure quality and consistency of color, and wear and to conduct tests at their in-house facility.

Warehousing and Shipping

Product batch lead times typically run two to four weeks, depending on the season and availability of the desired paint reactor. Burmese will supply approved packaging and shipping containers, and label the stock with labels supplied by the Company.

The Company can lease secured, scalable warehouse space at a reasonable rate in the same industrial complex where the paint factory is located. Loaded pallets are moved directly from the Burmese factory floor to the warehouse space by forklift, as part of the manufacturing price. Both facilities are secured, with fire suppression capabilities up to code. Each has contracts with several shipping firms that can handle DOT regulations.

Sales

The owner will sell the product line directly during the first two to three quarters. He expects to make 100 initial telephone calls per month for the first two months. Based on the potential size, interest, or test value to the Company, the owner will either follow up by phone, mail, e-mail, or direct contact. Once a routine has been established, a telemarketing firm will take over initial contact duties.

This process is expected to yield two or three sales, with an average volume of 150–400 gallons of LPS and/or Primer per month. The fiberglass lines are expected to average one or two sales per month, at an average net of approximately $250/sale. These sales are expected to build repeat volume over time. The owner will devote approximately 40 percent of his sales efforts to fiberglass repairs for at least nine months to see if he can create a market.

Orders will be taken only if they can be filled from existing inventory, or if a batch run's costs are fully covered by the customers' deposits or payments. No product will be shipped until the Company receives payment or verifies a customer's ability to pay.

Administrative Processes

The Company takes advantage of industry lead times, outside contractors, supplier contract funding, and outside technology arrangements to avoid administrative overhead. It uses a virtual office presence, an outside manufacturer and subcontractors, shippers, and suppliers.

All manufacturing, shipping, storage, testing, warehousing, accounting, and other functions are tracked on a notebook computer. The owner will take software classes and have a secured Web site built to permit taking orders from past customers, arrange shipments, and handle other business functions.

7. Management

The founder of the Company will oversee sales and operations in its early stages. This involves tracking costs, materials, and inventory, plus keeping track of product tests and sales.

If it is to grow, the Company needs a full-time manager and ultimately one person to run the office. The Company expects to hire an experienced business manager in the fourth quarter. In the second year, if not sooner, the Company will hire an office aide. In its second year the Company also will develop marketing and sales with manufacturers' representative firms to enable the owner to return to other duties.

The Company will hire

- a freelance business writer to develop product and sales literature, brochures, test results reports, and solicitation and business documents.
- an answering service to provide the business with a 24-hour virtual office presence, plus a other services.

Legal Counsel and Advisers

- The Company hired Drew & Coughlin, PC, to deal with contract matters and help negotiate agreements.
- Billing and payment transactions will be overseen by Cordelia Accounting, PC, which installed a custom software inventory control system in the Company's computer.
- The owner of a local paint store, who has paint manufacturing experience, has advised the Company, at no charge, on product testing and results.
- The owner has met several individuals in the industry—from labs to boardrooms—who regularly advise him on matters of importance.

8. Financial Analysis

First Year:

- Revenue assumptions
- Projected profits and loss (pro forma income statement)
- Cash flow analysis
- Projected balance sheet (pro forma balance sheet)

Supporting Documents

- Test results from state and federal testing organizations and agencies
- Manufacturing contract with Burmese Production Company of East St. Louis, Illinois
- Wholesale supply contract from a pool materials and equipment supplier for 400 gallons of LPS and 160 gallons of LPS Primer
- Sales purchase order from a marina in Florida for 25 pints of paste and 20 repair kits
- Signed contract to paint oil storage and separation tanks in Wyoming
- Owner's resume
- Test results, and photos and drawings from earlier product tests
- Research agreement with the testing laboratory
- Letter of compliance from the California Regional Air Quality Commission
- Copies of journal articles, reports, charts, or drawings from main information sources.

Luminous Paint Products Co.   **Combined Revenues/Cash Flow—Year One (Pro Forma)**

Month #	1	2	3	4	5	6	7	8	9	10	11	12	TOTALS
UNIT SALES													
Wholesale units sold													
LSP	520	530	557	585	292	585	614	307	614	645	322	645	6,216
LSP primer	240	245	250	255	127	260	265	130	265	270	284	270	2,861
Paste	24	24	25	25	26	26	27	28	28	29	29	30	322
Repair kits	5	5	5	5	5	6	6	6	6	6	6	6	67
Retail units sold													
LSP	200	210	221	232	122	243	255	134	268	281	295	310	2,771
LSP primer	160	168	176	185	97	194	204	107	214	225	236	248	2,217
Total gallons LSP	720	740	777	816	414	828	869	441	882	926	618	955	8,987
Total gallons primer	400	413	426	440	225	454	469	237	479	495	520	518	5,077
Total pints paste	24	24	25	25	26	26	27	28	28	29	29	30	322
Total repair	5	5	5	5	5	6	6	6	6	6	6	6	67

REVENUES (This section shown as a cash flow statement)

Wholesale — Full Pay

	1	2	3	4	5	6	7	8	9	10	11	12	TOTALS
LSP	$ 2,106	$ 2,148	$ 2,256	$ 2,368	$ 1,184	$ 2,368	$ 2,487	$ 1,243	$ 2,487	$ 2,611	$ 1,306	$ 2,611	$ 25,175
LSP primer	$ 756	$ 771	$ 787	$ 802	$ 401	$ 818	$ 835	$ 409	$ 835	$ 851	$ 894	$ 851	$ 9,011
Paste	$ 72	$ 73	$ 75	$ 76	$ 78	$ 79	$ 81	$ 83	$ 84	$ 86	$ 88	$ 90	$ 34,185
Repair kits	$ 21	$ 22	$ 22	$ 23	$ 23	$ 23	$ 24	$ 24	$ 25	$ 25	$ 26	$ 26	$ 285
Subtotal	$ 2,955	$ 3,014	$ 3,139	$ 3,270	$ 1,686	$ 3,290	$ 3,426	$ 1,760	$ 3,431	$ 3,574	$ 2,313	$ 3,578	$ 35,436

Wholesale — 30% Down

	1	2	3	4	5	6	7	8	9	10	11	12	TOTALS
LSP	$ 2,106	$ 2,148	$ 2,256	$ 2,368	$ 1,184	$ 2,368	$ 2,487	$ 1,243	$ 2,487	$ 2,611	$ 1,306	$ 2,611	$ 25,175
LSP primer	$ 756	$ 771	$ 787	$ 802	$ 401	$ 818	$ 835	$ 409	$ 835	$ 851	$ 894	$ 851	$ 9,011
Paste	$ 76	$ 77	$ 79	$ 80	$ 82	$ 83	$ 85	$ 87	$ 89	$ 90	$ 92	$ 94	$ 34,185
Repair kits	$ 19	$ 20	$ 20	$ 20	$ 21	$ 21	$ 22	$ 22	$ 22	$ 23	$ 23	$ 24	$ 257
Subtotal	$ 2,957	$ 3,016	$ 3,141	$ 3,271	$ 1,688	$ 3,291	$ 3,428	$ 1,761	$ 3,432	$ 3,576	$ 2,315	$ 3,580	$ 35,456

Wholesale — 70% Balance in 2 Months

	1	2	3	4	5	6	7	8	9	10	11	12	TOTALS
LSP		$ 4,914	$ 5,012	$ 5,263	$ 5,526	$ 2,763	$ 5,526	$ 5,802	$ 2,901	$ 5,802	$ 6,092		$ 49,603
LSP primer		$ 1,764	$ 1,799	$ 1,835	$ 1,872	$ 936	$ 1,909	$ 1,948	$ 955	$ 1,948	$ 1,987		$ 16,952
Paste		$ 176	$ 180	$ 184	$ 187	$ 191	$ 195	$ 199	$ 203	$ 207	$ 211		$ 1,932
Repair kits		$ 45	$ 46	$ 46	$ 47	$ 48	$ 49	$ 50	$ 51	$ 52	$ 53		$ 489
Subtotal		$ 6,899	$ 7,037	$ 7,328	$ 7,633	$ 3,938	$ 7,679	$ 7,999	$ 4,110	$ 8,009	$ 8,343		$ 68,975

Retail — Full Pay

	1	2	3	4	5	6	7	8	9	10	11	12	TOTALS
LSP	$ 6,318	$ 6,444	$ 6,767	$ 7,105	$ 3,552	$ 7,105	$ 7,460	$ 3,730	$ 7,460	$ 7,833	$ 3,917	$ 7,833	$ 75,524
LSP primer	$ 2,700	$ 2,754	$ 2,809	$ 2,865	$ 1,433	$ 2,923	$ 2,981	$ 1,461	$ 2,981	$ 3,041	$ 3,193	$ 3,041	$ 35,756
Subtotal	$ 9,018	$ 9,198	$ 9,576	$ 9,970	$ 4,985	$10,027	$10,441	$ 5,191	$10,441	$10,874	$ 7,109	$10,874	$107,705

Retail — 30% Down

	1	2	3	4	5	6	7	8	9	10	11	12	TOTALS
LSP	$ 2,106	$ 2,148	$ 2,256	$ 2,368	$ 1,184	$ 2,368	$ 2,487	$ 1,243	$ 2,487	$ 2,611	$ 1,306	$ 2,611	$ 25,175
LSP primer	$ 864	$ 881	$ 899	$ 917	$ 458	$ 935	$ 954	$ 468	$ 954	$ 973	$1,022	$ 973	$ 10,298
Subtotal	$ 2,970	$ 3,029	$ 3,154	$ 3,285	$ 1,643	$ 3,304	$ 3,441	$ 1,711	$ 3,441	$ 3,584	$ 2,327	$ 3,584	$ 35,473

Retail — 70% Balance in 2 Months

	1	2	3	4	5	6	7	8	9	10	11	12	TOTALS
LSP		$ 4,914	$ 5,012	$ 5,263	$ 5,526	$ 2,763	$ 5,526	$ 5,802	$ 2,901	$ 5,802	$ 6,092		$ 49,603
LSP primer		$ 2,016	$ 2,056	$ 2,097	$ 2,139	$ 1,070	$ 2,182	$ 2,226	$ 1,091	$ 2,226	$ 2,270		$ 19,374
Subtotal		$ 6,930	$ 7,069	$ 7,360	$ 7,665	$ 3,833	$ 7,708	$ 8,028	$ 3,992	$ 8,028	$ 8,363		$ 68,977

Luminous Paint Products Co. — Combined Revenues/Cash Flow—Year One (Pro Forma) (Continued)

Month #	1	2	3	4	5	6	7	8	9	10	11	12	TOTALS
GROSS SALES	$ 17,900	$ 18,258	$32,839	$33,902	$24,690	$35,210	$28,507	$25,811	$36,772	$29,709	$30,102	$38,322	$352,022
Manufacturing costs at 56%*	$ 10,024	$ 10,224	$18,390	$18,985	$13,826	$19,717	$15,964	$14,454	$20,592	$16,637	$16,857	$21,461	$197,132
Warehousing space	$ 200	$ 200	$ 200	$ 200	$ 200	$ 200	$ 200	$ 200	$ 200	$ 200	$ 200	$ 200	$ 2,400
**Sales/marketing costs	$ 4,046	$ 1,875	$ 1,347	$ 2,662	$ 1,154	$ 1,698	$ 1,868	$ 1,479	$ 2,145	$ 2,359	$ 2,595	$ 2,855	$ 26,083
Less cost of goods sold	$ 14,270	$ 12,299	$19,937	$21,847	$15,180	$21,615	$18,032	$16,133	$22,937	$19,196	$19,652	$24,516	$225,615
Gross margin	$ 3,630	$ 5,959	$12,902	$12,055	$ 9,510	$13,594	$10,475	$ 9,678	$13,835	$10,513	$10,450	$13,807	$126,407

*Manufacturing costs computed at 56% of sales

**Sales and marketing costs

	1	2	3	4	5	6	7	8	9	10	11	12	TOTALS
Graphic arts	$ 1,400												$ 1,400
Writer	$ 1,100	$ 650		$ 600									$ 600
Brochures, printing	$ 435			$ 580									$ 1,015
Travel/entertainment	$ 1,111	$ 1,225	$ 1,347	$ 1,482	$ 1,154	$ 1,698	$ 1,868	$ 1,479	$ 2,145	$ 2,359	$ 2,595	$ 2,855	$ 21,318
Subtotal	$ 4,046	$ 1,875	$ 1,347	$ 2,662	$ 1,154	$ 1,698	$ 1,868	$ 1,479	$ 2,145	$ 2,359	$ 2,595	$ 2,855	$ 26,083

General and Office Expenses

	1	2	3	4	5	6	7	8	9	10	11	12	TOTALS
Owner's salary	$ 2,000	$ 2,000	$ 2,000	$ 2,000	$ 2,000	$ 2,000	$ 2,000	$ 2,000	$ 2,000	$ 2,000	$ 2,000	$ 2,000	$ 24,000
General manager										$ 3,000	$ 3,000	$ 3,000	$ 9,000
Payroll burden	$ 700	$ 700	$ 700	$ 700	$ 700	$ 700	$ 700	$ 700	$ 700	$ 1,750	$ 1,750	$ 1,750	$ 11,550
Telephones	$ 90	$ 130	$ 143	$ 157	$ 173	$ 190	$ 209	$ 230	$ 253	$ 279	$ 307	$ 337	$ 2,499
Answering service	$ 225	$ 225	$ 225	$ 225	$ 225	$ 225	$ 225	$ 225	$ 225	$ 225	$ 225	$ 225	$ 2,700
Internet connection	$ 25	$ 25	$ 25	$ 25	$ 25	$ 25	$ 25	$ 25	$ 25	$ 25	$ 25	$ 25	$ 300
Computer lease	$ 99	$ 99	$ 99	$ 99	$ 99	$ 99	$ 99	$ 99	$ 99	$ 99	$ 99	$ 99	$ 1,188
Printer	$ 475												$ 475
Web site	$ 1,900	$ 750											$ 2,650
Web site space lease	$ 40	$ 40	$ 40	$ 40	$ 40	$ 40	$ 40	$ 40	$ 40	$ 40	$ 40	$ 40	$ 480
Custom software package	$ 1,200												$ 1,200
Legal	$ 2,500												$ 2,500
Insurance	$ 230	$ 230	$ 230	$ 230	$ 230	$ 230	$ 230	$ 230	$ 230	$ 230	$ 230	$ 230	$ 2,760
Subtotal general & office	$ 9,484	$ 4,199	$ 3,462	$ 3,476	$ 3,492	$ 3,509	$ 3,528	$ 3,549	$ 3,572	$ 7,648	$ 7,676	$ 7,706	$ 61,302
Gross margin	$ 3,630	$ 5,959	$12,902	$12,055	$ 9,510	$13,594	$10,475	$ 9,678	$13,835	$10,513	$10,450	$13,807	$126,407
Less general & office	$ 9,484	$ 4,199	$ 3,462	$ 3,476	$ 3,492	$ 3,509	$ 3,528	$ 3,549	$ 3,572	$ 7,648	$ 7,676	$ 7,706	$ 61,302
Net profit before taxes	$ (5,854)	$ 1,760	$ 9,440	$ 8,578	$ 6,018	$10,085	$ 6,947	$ 6,129	$10,262	$ 2,865	$ 2,774	$ 6,101	$ 65,105
Running monthly balance	$ (5,854)	$ (4,095)	$ 5,346	$13,924	$19,942	$30,027	$36,973	$43,102	$53,364	$56,230	$59,004	$65,105	
Taxes	$ (5,854)	$ (1,433)	$ 2,802	$ 3,002	$ 2,106	$ 3,530	$ 2,431	$ 2,145	$ 3,592	$ 1,003	$ 971	$ 2,135	$ 16,431
Net profit	$ (5,854)	$ (3,193)	$ 6,638	$ 5,576	$ 3,911	$ 6,555	$ 4,515	$ 3,984	$ 6,670	$ 1,863	$ 1,803	$ 3,965	$ 42,820

Assumptions

1. First month sales of LSP, primer, paste and repair kits are actual sales.
2. Wholesale growth in sales for all four products projected at 2% per month.
3. Retail growth in sales for two products projected at 5% per month.
4. All deposit sales shown at 30% down, balance after 60 days.
5. Deposit sales = 75% of Wholesale, 50% of Retail.
6. Wholesale unit prices: LSP = $18, Primer = $14, Paste = $14, Repair kits = $17.
7. Retail unit prices: LSP = $27, Primer = $25.
8. All sales paid in advance receive a 10% discount.
9. No discounts shown for purchase volumes.
10. No sales are projected for repeat/referral orders.
11. Direct manufacturing costs are shown as 56% of sales.
12. Manufacturing process prices come from the Burmese price list.
13. Taxes shown at 25%.

Computer Training Services, Inc.

Executive Summary

Computing Training Services (CTS) is a new company that will be built on the experience of its founder to take advantage of the growing need for computer training. The founder, Steve Omar, brings almost 15 years of computer training expertise to the business. He will establish the Company as a high quality, computer training service provider in the Miami, Florida, metropolitan area.

In its first six months, Computing Training Services will offer courses of instruction for integrated Microsoft products. In the second six-month period, CTS also will begin offering classes on creating and maintaining Web sites.

Computer training is a continuing process, especially for small businesses. New programs are developed, more powerful revisions are issued, and new hires in all companies are a constant in our business world. CTS will differentiate itself from its competitors (generally larger firms) through lower pricing and the use of a proprietary set of electronic workbooks that serve as training aids and reference guides. Additionally, the Company has established a strategic alliance with several computer resellers to offer their customers the added benefit of training.

The Business

Company Overview

CTS is a newly formed Florida corporation, incorporated in December 1998. It is wholly owned by Steve Omar. CTS will establish its initial operations in Miami, Florida. CTS intends to offer computer training courses for several software packages that have been almost universally accepted by small- to medium-size businesses and by many individuals. A new course, currently under development, will provide instruction on how to create and maintain Web sites on the Internet, and will be launched in the second half of 1999.

The owner and principal employee, Steve Omar, has extensive experience as branch manager of the computer training and development department of Staffing Pros, Inc. In addition, Mr. Omar has developed a marketing strategy that should prove attractive to the small- to mid-size business market.

The Service

CTS was created for the sole purpose of providing computer software training services in the Miami metropolitan area. The courses in Microsoft Windows 95/98, Excel, Word, Access, and PowerPoint are designed to provide employees and owners of small businesses with the skills they need to work efficiently in a computerized business environment. Training in Web site development and maintenance, to be offered in the second six months, will enable small businesses to establish their own Internet presence for business marketing and promotional purposes.

The training courses generally will be offered at a rented facility located in Miami. The facility is easily accessible, has substantial parking, and is served by public transportation. Where appropriate, CTS will provide training at a customer's facility.

CTS has designed a program that offers its clients several key benefits:

- Training for most desirable/compatible programs
- 16–20-hour classes
- Electronic workbooks
- Aggressive pricing
- Convenient location
- Multiple class times

The Classes

CTS has chosen to limit its training to software programs developed by Microsoft. It believes that by limiting its training to what is considered the most popular interrelated family of products that it can offer its customers the highest degree of user benefit. Software programs will include:

- *Windows 95/98*. The basic operating program for Microsoft products
- *Word*. A highly developed word processing program
- *Excel*. A sophisticated spreadsheet program
- *Access*. A database program for developing mail lists and other business information systems
- *PowerPoint*. A program for developing and making sales presentations

All of these programs are easily interrelated and are capable of accepting and fully integrating input from each other. The Company will offer two class packages:

1. A one-course, 12-hour, single software program class for $155
2. Three courses, a 24 hour, integrated class covering three related, software programs for $325

Each class, one-day and three-day, has two levels: beginner and advanced. Each level costs the same price.

The Workbooks

One method that CTS will use to distinguish its training courses from those offered by other companies is a group of electronic workbooks developed by Mr. Omar. These workbooks, one for each application, will serve as a training aid during sessions, and as a valuable reference tool thereafter. The workbooks incorporate ideas and concepts proven successful during Mr. Omar's tenure at Staffing Pros, coupled with innovative new concepts developed as a result of his insight into Staffing Pros' training operations.

The workbooks will be provided to CTS students on CD-ROM. Each workbook approaches the software as a user would, but brings them up the learning curve faster than any tutorial can. The material in each workbook is laid out in a logical and easy-to-follow format. It clearly illustrates the commonly used features of each application, and provides numerous examples and shortcuts that apply to a variety of different business and personal situations.

The Market

Overview

Computer training is in a period of continual expansion according to the findings of several respected industry trade journals. Because of the great technological innovations being made in personal and business application software and the impact of the Internet on daily life, many individuals and businesses are finding themselves overwhelmed with the possibilities that these new business tools offer.

Mr. Omar conducted competitive research prior to forming CTS. The focus of this research was on the growth of computer training in general and on the geographic market he plans to serve. As an example, the Management and Decision Information Systems Institute (MDISI) conducted a national study of small business training needs. The study indicates that 85 percent of 1,500 business owners polled anticipated an immediate need to have one or more employees trained in the use of the popular spreadsheet and wordprocessing software packages developed by Microsoft. Thus, the findings of the MDISI study are useful in establishing the number of potential students that CTS might serve.

According to a recent article in *PC World*, "because the need for computer literacy is rising, the demand for PC training and education is also growing. Whether they hire computer training centers or have their own in-house training program, local companies are realizing that investing in hardware is not enough. For a firm to truly be in the information technology mainstream, it must invest in its most precious resource, its people."

Competitive Profile

In the greater Miami area, information compiled by the Chamber of Commerce reveals that 20 thousand businesses are classified as small- to medium-size (one to 50 employees). The average number of employees is 15. This means that in the business market that CTS plans to serve, there are approximately 300 thousand potential students.

By implementing a marketing strategy that stresses quality training at an economical price, the Company believes it will be successful in capturing a significant portion of the target market from the larger, more expensive, regional and national training firms. By offering the same or higher quality training at a cost 25 percent less than the larger chains, and by offering its exclusive electronic workbooks, CTS will be perceived as being a quality training provider in step with the information, time, and budgetary needs of small- to medium-size businesses.

Management believes that through its strategic alliances with computer resellers, it will be able to successfully market to individual users and their families. Combining both markets in the same classes creates economies of scale in using instructor services.

Marketing Strategy

CTS will market itself as offering higher quality, user-friendly computer training at a more reasonable price than its competitors. CTS will sell to the small business market by emphasizing value and by identifying with their information, time, and budgetary needs.

Pricing Strategy

CTS will charge significantly less for training services than the larger computer training firms. CTS will have lower overhead expenses and fewer employees than the larger firms. Based on a telephone survey and personal knowledge of computer training firms in Miami and its surrounding suburbs, competitive training firms charge, on the average, $220 per person for a 12-hour training session in Microsoft Word or Excel. At

CTS, for approximately $450, a student can receive three 12-hour sessions that includes basic computing, Word, and Excel.

To appeal to the cost conscious small business owner, CTS anticipates offering a 12-hour training session in Windows 95/98, Excel, and Word (or WordPerfect) for $155 to beginners. Individual classes in Access and PowerPoint will be offered at $120. Advanced classes for these software packages will be offered for $165 per student. A total package, including beginning or advanced training in Windows 95/98, Word, and Excel, will be offered for $325. This represents a substantial discount over the competition, regardless of whether clients select training in a single software application or training in multiple applications.

Advertising

CTS will advertise in the local daily newspaper, plus several local small business and home office magazines. The *Miami Herald* will run a small display ad in its Friday, Saturday, and Sunday Business sections for $1,200 per month. In particular, Mr. Omar has received reasonable advertising estimates from *Miami Business Monthly*. For $250 per month, *Miami Small Business Monthly* will run a half-page ad. After the initial 12-month period, CTS is also considering running a full-page ad for $350 per month in the *Miami Home Computing Journal*.

Promotional

The preferred mode of advertising is word-of-mouth. In addition, Mr. Omar has begun writing several articles for local business publications. Research results in the MDISI report suggests that this type of marketing initiative can generate a reasonable amount of business through referrals.

Strategic Alliances

CTS intends to utilize the contacts generated by its strategic relationships with several local computer resellers. These resellers believe that by offering CTS training, they will gain a competitive advantage over other dealers and mail order sellers.

Sales

Mr. Omar will also approach business owners in person to identify their computing needs and how he might satisfy them. Mr. Omar will utilize his own experience, training, and understanding of clients' needs to generate new clients and keep the old ones. He will not rely on a sales force to generate business.

Owner and Key Personnel

Initial staffing will be kept to a minimum using the cross-over talents of three persons.

Steve Omar is the owner and manager of CTS. He has significant computer software experience and management skills developed as the manager of the Technical Support and Training group for Large Corporation, Inc. He plans to utilize this experience in preparing and presenting computer training programs.

Mr. Omar was a technical support technician and in-house training instructor for eight years before becoming manager of training three years ago. He holds degrees in both education and electrical engineering. As the manager for Large Corporation, Mr. Omar coordinated a staff of five instructors who trained company employees in various Microsoft software packages such as Word, Excel, PowerPoint, and Windows 95. Mr. Omar also taught a number of these courses. Utilizing this experience, Mr. Omar will coordinate the training efforts of a part-time instructor and a training assistant in order to provide CTS's students with the greatest amount of access to the training personnel.

Because Mr. Omar has a technical background which includes the servicing of computer hardware, computer downtime will be minimized because Mr. Omar can make at least minor repairs rather than waiting for a computer technician.

JoAnn Stills. Ms. Stills will work part-time and function as a training and office assistant. She has five years of experience working as an office manager for a large computer training firm as well as extensive training in the most common software packages. This training will provide a benefit to CTS when the instructors need some extra help with larger classes. CTS is employing Ms. Stills to run the office and help out in the larger training classes assisting the instructors.

Ms. Sue Johnson, who is an independent contractor, will function as an additional computer trainer for evening classes and weekends. Ms. Johnson also has received extensive training that will allow her to review and evaluate new software and network products. While working at Large Corporation, she earned a certificate as a Microsoft Certified Systems Engineer. As a result she has developed expertise in planning, implementing, maintaining, and supporting information systems including Microsoft Windows NT, BackOffice, and various other server software. In addition, she has earned training certificates from the Institute for Technology Training in Microsoft Word, Windows, Excel, PowerPoint and Windows 95/98.

Board of Advisers

Joe Thomason, manager of national computer reseller
Sally Smart, local community college computer instructor
Phil Wray, vice president of Small Business Affairs, Miami Community Bank & Trust Company

Operations

Training Facility

The company plans to generate most of its income through large classroom training sessions. This is more advantageous because it involves almost the same amount of work for the trainer to teach a group as it does to teach an individual. Obviously, group settings generate a much larger amount of training revenues at one time. For example, even if CTS doubled its single application tuition from $155 to $310 to provide on-site training, it would still generate less revenue than the $1,550 that CTS would make training 10 students at the same time at $155 per student.

CTS has negotiated a favorable lease in a strip center. CTS has a three-year lease with a three-year renewal option. The monthly rent is $1,500 for the first year, $1,700 the second year, and $1,900 for the third year.

During the three-year renewal period, rent will increase by 5 percent per year. This rental amount includes utilities, waste removal, and all maintenance costs. Initial physical layout is quickly adaptable to two classrooms accommodating up to 25 students each. Third and forth rooms will require reasonable leasehold improvements. The facility also contains four smaller offices for staff and ample power connections for multiple computer equipment is available.

To demonstrate a presence, CTS will accommodate a limited number of clients by offering on-site training to corporations, at a premium price. Pricing for this type of training will be provided on a contract basis because the variables may include not only numbers of students but also the availability of computers.

Computer Equipment

After an analysis of the financial and other implications of buying, renting, or leasing, CTS has decided to lease its computers and printers. A factor that played a large part in that decision was the likelihood that purchased equipment would become obsolete in a relatively short period of time, plus the fact that many of its students may be working with newer equipment. CTS must have available computers that are at least equal in sophistication to those used by its customers. The substantial initial cash outlay required to purchase 15 to 30 computers also played a part in the decision to lease or rent.

The lease would run for 12 months, renewable annually for three years, at an 11 percent annual interest rate. The total of the 36 monthly payments would be $120,000. A new generation of computers would be available in each yearly period for an additional one-time 15 percent fee in the year in which the lease was rolled over. The lease payment deal of $3,854 per month for 30 computers and six printers is $1,250 less than the monthly rental alternative.

Software was licensed for use on 30 computers for $18,500. This purchase was financed over three years for a monthly payment of $596. The owner estimates that updates and new software in subsequent years will cost an additional $300 per month.

Tuition Collection

CTS will require that a nonrefundable 25 percent deposit be sent when a student registers for classes. Full payment will be required at the time a student shows up for class. Payments for classes may be made with cash, credit cards, or personal checks. CTS will offer deferred monthly billing to those corporate clients with five or more employees in attendance.

Financial Information

Expenses

After salaries, the cost of computers and the cost of obtaining a training facility will be the largest expenses that CTS will face. Detailed two-year projections are included.

Revenue Assumptions

Based on a survey of 100 computer training firms in Miami, Mobile, Tallahasee, and Memphis, it was determined that a computer training facility with one full-time and at least two part-time staff members can be expect to train 24 new students every week. Of this number, it is expected that 25 percent will be repeat customers. That means that CTS can reasonably expect to generate 96 new students and 24 repeat students per month, after classes start in its second month.

The percentage breakdown of the number of students who will select either a single course or the total package is based on statistics provided in the MDISI study and a report included in *The Journal of Computer Training and Development*, May 1999. The findings of both of these reports reflect the fact that individuals who have taken previous computer training courses are more likely to pursue additional training to gain even greater proficiency and expertise in different software applications.

After revising these statistics, based on the owner's personal experience, CTS estimates that gross revenue in the first year will be $345,400, or an average of $29,000 per month. This monthly estimate can be broken down as follows:

- 80 percent of new students take a single software package course costing $155.
- 20 percent of new students take the three-course package costing $325.
- 10 percent of former students take one additional software course (at $155) after 3 months.
- 15 percent of former students take one three-course package (at $325) after 3 months.
- Tuition will be taken in the month when the student starts class.

Based on discussions with a number of vendors that provide software to computer training firms, a computer training business just starting up can expect at least a 15 percent to 20 percent monthly increase in student enrollment in year two over year one. Accordingly, CTS is planning for a 15 percent increase in student enrollment in year two. For a detailed analysis of the actual monthly gross income for the first year of operation, review the profit and loss statements provided in the financial projection section.

CTS Computer Training Services
Year One Pro Forma

Month #	1	2	3	4	5	6	7	8	9	10	11	12	TOTALS
REVENUES													
New 1-course		$14,880	$15,178	$15,481	$15,791	$16,107	$16,429	$16,757	$17,092	$17,434	$17,783	$18,139	$181,070
New 3-courses		$ 7,800	$ 7,956	$ 8,115	$ 8,277	$ 8,443	$ 8,612	$ 8,784	$ 8,960	$ 9,139	$ 9,322	$ 9,508	$ 94,916
Former +1-course					$ 1,488	$ 1,518	$ 1,548	$ 1,579	$ 1,611	$ 1,643	$ 1,676	$ 1,709	$ 12,771
Former +3-courses					$ 4,680	$ 4,774	$ 4,869	$ 4,966	$ 5,066	$ 5,167	$ 5,270	$ 5,376	$ 40,168
Referral 1-course				$ 372	$ 379	$ 387	$ 395	$ 403	$ 411	$ 419	$ 427	$ 436	$ 3,629
Referral 3-courses				$ 195	$ 199	$ 203	$ 207	$ 211	$ 215	$ 220	$ 224	$ 228	$ 1,902
Web course						$ 930	$ 1,550	$ 1,860	$ 2,325	$ 2,325	$ 1,860		$ 10,850
Gross revenues		$22,680	$23,134	$24,163	$30,815	$31,431	$32,989	$34,251	$35,215	$36,347	$37,027	$37,256	$345,307
Direct costs*		$ 5,601	$ 5,637	$ 5,674	$ 5,712	$ 5,752	$ 5,793	$ 5,836	$ 5,880	$ 5,926	$ 5,974	$ 6,023	$ 63,808
Net revenue		$17,079	$17,497	$18,490	$25,102	$25,679	$27,196	$28,415	$29,334	$30,421	$31,054	$31,234	$281,500
EXPENSES													
Direct Costs													
Course manuals and handouts		$ 672	$ 699	$ 727	$ 756	$ 786	$ 818	$ 850	$ 884	$ 920	$ 956	$ 995	$ 9,063
CD-ROM workbooks		$ 454	$ 463	$ 472	$ 481	$ 491	$ 501	$ 511	$ 521	$ 531	$ 542	$ 553	$ 5,520
Computer/printer lease		$ 3,854	$ 3,854	$ 3,854	$ 3,854	$ 3,854	$ 3,854	$ 3,854	$ 3,854	$ 3,854	$ 3,854	$ 3,854	$42,394
Software payment		$ 596	$ 596	$ 596	$ 596	$ 596	$ 596	$ 596	$ 596	$ 596	$ 596	$ 596	$ 6,556
Classroom supplies		$ 25	$ 25	$ 25	$ 25	$ 25	$ 25	$ 25	$ 25	$ 25	$ 25	$ 25	$ 25
Total direct cost of sales		$ 5,601	$ 5,637	$ 5,674	$ 5,712	$ 5,752	$ 5,793	$ 5,836	$ 5,880	$ 5,926	$ 5,974	$ 6,023	$63,808
Sales and Marketing Expenses													
Advertising/ promotion	$ 1,680	$ 1,680	$ 1,680	$ 1,680	$ 1,680	$ 1,680	$ 1,680	$ 1,680	$ 1,680	$ 1,680	$ 1,680	$ 1,680	$20,160
Brochures	$ 800						$ 1,000						$ 1,800
Meals/ entertainment	$ 150	$ 150	$ 150	$ 150	$ 150	$ 150	$ 150	$ 150	$ 150	$ 150	$ 150	$ 150	$ 1,800
Mileage (for owner)	$ 50	$ 50	$ 50	$ 50	$ 50	$ 50	$ 50	$ 50	$ 50	$ 50	$ 50	$ 50	$ 600
Total sales and marketing	$ 2,680	$ 1,880	$ 1,880	$ 1,880	$ 1,880	$ 1,880	$ 2,880	$ 1,880	$ 1,880	$ 1,880	$ 1,880	$ 1,880	$ 24,360
Personnel Expenses													
Steve Omar	$ 2,500	$ 2,500	$ 2,500	$ 2,500	$ 2,500	$ 2,500	$ 2,500	$ 2,500	$ 2,500	$ 2,500	$ 2,500	$ 2,500	$ 30,000
Ms. Johnson	$ 2,815	$ 2,815	$ 2,815	$ 2,815	$ 2,815	$ 2,815	$ 2,815	$ 2,815	$ 2,815	$ 2,815	$ 2,815	$ 2,815	$ 33,780
Ms. Stills	$ 2,165	$ 2,165	$ 2,165	$ 2,165	$ 2,165	$ 2,165	$ 2,165	$ 2,165	$ 2,165	$ 2,165	$ 2,165	$ 2,165	$ 25,980
Total salaries	$ 7,480	$ 7,480	$ 7,480	$ 7,480	$ 7,480	$ 7,480	$ 7,480	$ 7,480	$ 7,480	$ 7,480	$ 7,480	$ 7,480	$ 89,760
Benefits and payroll burden	$ 2,618	$ 2,618	$ 2,618	$ 2,618	$ 2,618	$ 2,618	$ 2,618	$ 2,618	$ 2,618	$ 2,618	$ 2,618	$ 2,618	$ 31,416
Total personnel expenses	$10,098	$10,098	$10,098	$10,098	$10,098	$10,098	$10,098	$10,098	$10,098	$10,098	$10,098	$10,098	$121,176

CTS Computer Training Services (Continued)
Year One Pro Forma

Month #	1	2	3	4	5	6	7	8	9	10	11	12	TOTALS
General and Office Expenses													
Office lease	$ 3,000	$ 1,500	$ 1,500	$ 1,500	$ 1,500	$ 1,500	$ 1,500	$ 1,500	$ 1,500	$ 1,500	$ 1,500	$ 1,500	$ 9,500
Leaseholder improvements	$ 6,300												$ 6,300
Install electrical cabling	$ 4,100												$ 4,100
Telephones	$ 105	$ 60	$ 60	$ 60	$ 60	$ 60	$ 60	$ 60	$ 60	$ 60	$ 60	$ 60	$ 765
Answering service	$ 220	$ 220	$ 220	$ 220	$ 220	$ 220	$ 220	$ 220	$ 220	$ 220	$ 220	$ 220	$ 2,640
Internet connection	$ 25	$ 25	$ 25	$ 25	$ 25	$ 25	$ 50	$ 50	$ 50	$ 50	$ 50	$ 50	$ 450
Office complete with read/ write CD	$ 1,400												$ 1,400
Office furniture (used)	$ 450												$ 450
Classroom furnishings	$ 4,200												$ 4,200
Decoration	$ 900												$ 900
Stationery family	$ 350												$ 350
Graphic arts	$ 1,000												$ 1,000
Legal	$ 3,500												$ 3,500
Insurance	$ 70	$ 70	$ 70	$ 70	$ 70	$ 70	$ 70	$ 70	$ 70	$ 70	$ 70	$ 70	$ 840
Printing/ computer typesetting	$ 980												$ 980
Trade journals/ teaching material	$ 75	$ 75	$ 75	$ 75	$ 75	$ 75	$ 75	$ 75	$ 75	$ 75	$ 75	$ 75	$ 900
Total general and office expense	$ 26,675	$ 1,950	$ 1,950	$ 1,950	$ 1,950	$ 1,950	$ 1,975	$ 1,975	$ 1,975	$ 1,975	$ 1,975	$ 1,975	$ 48,275

Balance

	1	2	3	4	5	6	7	8	9	10	11	12	TOTALS
Net revenues	—	$ 17,079	$ 17,497	$ 18,490	$ 25,102	$ 25,679	$ 27,196	$ 28,415	$ 29,334	$ 30,421	$ 31,054	$ 31,234	$ 281,500
Sales and marketing	$ 2,680	$ 1,880	$ 1,880	$ 1,880	$ 1,880	$ 1,880	$ 2,880	$ 1,880	$ 1,880	$ 1,880	$ 1,880	$ 1,880	$ 24,360
Personnel expenses	$ 10,098	$ 10,098	$ 10,098	$ 10,098	$ 10,098	$ 10,098	$ 10,098	$ 10,098	$ 10,098	$ 10,098	$ 10,098	$ 10,098	$ 121,176
General and administrative	$ 26,675	$ 1,950	$ 1,950	$ 1,950	$ 1,950	$ 1,950	$ 1,975	$ 1,975	$ 1,975	$ 1,975	$ 1,975	$ 1,975	$ 48,275
Total expenses	$ 39,453	$ 13,928	$ 13,928	$ 13,928	$ 13,928	$ 13,928	$ 14,953	$ 13,953	$ 13,953	$ 13,953	$ 13,953	$ 13,953	$ 193,811
Net income before taxes	$(39,453)	$ 3,151	$ 3,569	$ 4,562	$ 11,174	$ 11,751	$ 12,243	$ 14,462	$ 15,381	$ 16,468	$ 17,101	$ 17,281	$ 87,689
Taxes		$(36,302)	$(32,733)	$(28,171)	$(16,997)	$(5,246)	$ 2,449	$ 5,062	$ 5,383	$ 5,764	$ 5,985	$ 6,048	$ 30,691
Net profit	$(39,453)	$ 3,151	$ 3,569	$ 4,562	$ 11,174	$ 11,751	$ 9,794	$ 9,400	$ 9,998	$ 10,704	$ 11,115	$ 11,232	$ 56,998

Assumptions

Manuals created in-house. 1-course @$4.00 each, 3-course @ $12.00 each
CD-ROM costs = 2% of gross revenues
Answering service includes other office services, conference room rental for two to four hours/month
Legal expense covers incorporation, education, and employment contracts
Benefits at 35%
Taxes at 35%

Construction Delivery Corporation
Business Plan

Executive Summary

Mission Statement

To deliver construction project CAD blueprints and specifications to the computers of contractors, engineers, and architects over a high-quality, secure online subscriber network, at the lowest possible cost.

Company and History

The Company was incorporated in California in August 1998. Feasibility studies and technical research was conducted from January 1998 to incorporation.

Company Overview

Every day, contractors, subcontractors, engineers, and architects all over the country review endless reams of paper construction blueprints and specification books. It's a required but frustrating, time-consuming and expensive process in the effort to build buildings, design and install systems, and prepare estimates and bids for construction projects.

The paper blueprint process has been done this way for centuries. The people who need to review these multiple and complex pieces of paper are used to doing this by going to plan rooms where they review and often copy what they need, or alternatively, purchase full sets of plans and specifications for review back in their offices.

The Company takes these difficult-to-handle plans and specifications and puts them where they belong—on the bidding company's computer. Delivery is accomplished via a private online subscriber network (Extranet)—that feeds directly to the office desktop monitors of architects, engineers, contractors, and other industry professionals.

Customers have instant access, 24 hours a day, seven days a week. Original architectural/engineering computer aided design (CAD) blueprints and specifications for all projects for bid—public and private—are available on the network. Timely industry news and features are available to subscribers each morning. These include daily project specification updates, new project alerts, and results of project bids and awards. Key construction industry Web sites are linked on the Company's home page.

Revenue is based on monthly subscriber fees. Pricing is tiered according to level and extent of service desired by the subscribing company client.

The current market is open, with little direct competition. The project is global in its implications. The construction industry has openly admitted it is "in the stone age" in information technology, and has vowed to embrace projects like this because of the huge savings to them in time and money.

Goals and Objectives

- To provide "on screen" dimension and material takeoffs (measurements) that dramatically increase the speed and accuracy of the bid and estimating process for Company subscribers.
- To be the major, early facilitator in moving construction blueprints and specs from paper to an easy-to-use, high-speed online subscriber network.
- To provide instant access to CAD plans and specs for network subscribers in their individual service territories, over a secured online system.
- To enable each client the opportunity to bid on many more major construction contracts per month.
- To dominate construction industry online network information services.
- Strong earnings commensurate with the highest quality management practices and customer-oriented philosophy and practice.

Industry Overview

NOTE: *The term* contractors *as used in this summary business plan includes general contractors and subcontractors like plumbing, electrical, heating, ventilating and air-conditioning (HVAC), or landscaping, lighting, and many other specialty subcontractors. It can also include suppliers to these contractors such as manufacturer's representatives for door frames, locks and hardware, electrical switches, lights and wiring, plumbing piping, drains and fixtures, roofing materials, building steel, and reinforcing and joists. The list is almost endless.*

According to trade journal articles and interviews with selected associations, four million companies operate within the U.S. construction industry. These include contractors, suppliers, and a variety of specialty firms and jobbers.

Contractors spend hour after hour trying to chase down blueprints and specs of projects on which they may want to bid. In some cases they must go directly to the offices of architects, engineers, building owners, or project managers. In many cases, they go to plan rooms which contain the plans and specs for projects in their region. The contractors pay a monthly fee to access these plan rooms and additional fees for copies of the plan sheets or specs that apply to their particular needs. They may travel many miles across a congested urban area to review these plans.

Once they get to the plan rooms, the problems can intensify. Scanning and copy equipment might be down. There may be no one there to help and assist them. Most plan rooms are open only during business hours—no nights, holidays, or weekends. This can prevent contractors from reviewing projects when the time is convenient for them. Lost jobs may be the result. Often, construction project updates and changes are released and the contractors must attempt to visit, sometimes daily, to keep informed. If they don't stay on top of changes, this can cause inaccurate bidding and estimating, and contracts lost to competitors. The system is antiquated and unruly, and ends up being very expensive compared to the online network alternative offered by the Company

"Takeoffs"—Measuring and Estimating Quantities of Materials

In printed form, construction blueprint sets are bulky, complex, and unwieldy—not easy to use. Once a contractor has a set of blueprints for a project on which it may want to bid, it must perform material and dimension takeoffs (measurements) directly from the plans.

In many instances, contractors may be concerned only with certain elements of the project such as, heating and ventilating, or electrical systems. In the paper-based blueprint process, contractors are forced to buy a complete set of plans, where the cost for full blueprint sets can deter them from even bidding on certain projects.

The process is slow, tedious, and often results in inaccurate estimates. Common practice is to use a ruler or scale, measure, record and calculate the qualities. Inexperienced estimators can end up "lost" in this process.

Primary and Potential Competition

Associated General Contractors Association (AGC). This group is located in every city of size across the country. Local contractors belong and the organization supplies many benefits from local to national lobbying to plan rooms. These plan rooms are one of the primary sources for assembling plans and specifications for projects in an area. Almost every potential customer of the Company currently is a member of its local AGC.

F. W. Dodge plan rooms. This large national company offers online access to selected large project blueprints and specifications. Its program does not have online estimating capabilities and it does not offer local project plans. The very high cost of service leaves out most construction companies.

Construction software companies. It could be that premier software companies such as Autodesk might look into entering online plan room services to compete with the Company's. However, this would be a new business for them—uncharted territory.

Large companies. A company such as McGraw-Hill, producer of online and newsstand construction periodicals, may want to look into entering the online plan room market. This would be a new business for them, too.

Trade associations. More aggressive trade associations such as the American Institute of Architects may want to look into offering some form of online plan service to its members.

Reprographic plan rooms have been slow to convert to, or even investigate, online plan rooms. They have had strong revenues based on scanning and copying—paper based services. They are reluctant to retool and enter what is a new field for them—high-tech online plan rooms. They don't want to spend the money. And, in many cases, they are unaware of the coming high-tech changes.

Competitive Advantage

Company management has identified a major misconception on the part of potential competitors. There is a common belief that architects and engineers will not volunteer their proprietary CAD designs and plans to be placed on a network for all subscribers to see. This is a distinct edge for the moment, because it is not true. Architects and engineers are supportive of the Company's system because they say it will make their jobs easier. They like the idea that with their plans on the network, more contractors will see and bid on their projects. More competition will result in reduced costs to architects' clients—public and private. And, they say, intellectual theft can occur in any existing plan room now—though they say this is not a widespread problem. The Company's management has met with numerous architects and engineers, who, after hearing its presentation say things like: "Great idea! How can we help?"

Unlike others, the Company is focused on one major business. If there is a project out there for bid, they will have it available online for subscribers to review and to perform material and dimension takeoffs. All projects, public and private, big and small.

- Open 24 hours a day, seven days a week.
- Skilled sales force.
- Personal contact with customers on a continuous basis.

Product and Service

The Blueprint Delivery™ Service

The Company has devised a proprietary software system operating on a Windows NT server platform, called "Delivery." The Delivery™ Service makes the bidding from blueprint process much easier and faster by enabling precise, on-screen takeoffs over a secure, password-protected Extranet (a secure section of a Web site that only visitors with passwords can enter).

Using a mouse and electronic drawings or a digitizer and paper plans, the user simply "traces" over the items needing to be calculated. He or she can zoom in for a closer look, calculate lineal and/or square footage, count objects, takeoff roof pitches, measure beams, etc. Floors, ceilings, walls, plumbing, electrical, bricks, etc., are all automatically computed.

Users can switch from English to metric systems and back again. No more scale errors, miscalculations, overlooked materials. Totaling quantities means simply exporting them into the Company's custom program or the customer's favorite spreadsheet. Bid completion is fast, efficient, and cost saving.

The Company's system includes the following features, some of which are proprietary:

- Computer Aided Design (CAD) software, including dimension and material takeoff capability: Autodesk/AutoCAD, and others being added.
- Online subscriber payment capability available by credit cards.
- A T-1, with two backup T-3 lines, operating on ASDL (Asynchronous Digital Lines) for better high-speed service connectivity. Most blueprints can be downloaded in one minute or less.
- Virtual Private Network (VPN) technology for subscriber companies selecting Intranet service for secure information exchanges within their company and with employees in the field or satellite offices.
- Multiple redundant network security systems to prevent unauthorized entries or changes to blueprints.

Marketing

The Market

The construction industry plays a significant part in any economy—local, regional, or national. It starts with planners and runs down to the food trucks that serve worker lunches on site.

The commercial, industrial, and government markets for new construction and expansion exceeded $400 billion in 1998. In the first two quarters of the year, new home construction projects ran over $40 billion. Commercial construction passed $100 billion. Industrial and business expansion projects passed the $250 billion mark.

Key Marketing Points

The Company offers several unique selling points over its competition:

- Blueprints on your desktop monitor—not all over your office.
- Chase contracts—not blueprints.
- With the Company's system, the client wins more jobs because they identify jobs on the network they wouldn't otherwise have known about.
- The Company's plan room is open 24 hours a day, seven days a week.
- Expanded bidding capacity. The Delivery System opens the door to regional, national, and international bids. Firms who previously did not bid on projects now can do so.

A case example. A contractor needs to see the plans, released yesterday, for a proposed new elementary school in San Mateo, California. Contractor: "I need to take a look at this job. I have some time, and it's at the end of a long day. But by the time I get to XYZ Plan Room on Highway 2 they'll probably be closed. Plus, it's Friday. Well, maybe if I hurry I can get there. Oh yeah, their copier was down on Monday when I was there. I wonder if they fixed it? I better call first to see if they even have the plans yet. Bet they don't."

To this "universal contractor," the Company says: Put your truck keys in your pocket, lock the front door, grab a soda, and sit down in front of your desktop monitor. Call up the Company's online Network site, enter your password, click on "New Elementary School, City, State," and point and click your way through the entire project.

Want to send it to your home system to look through it over the weekend? Go ahead. You have the unique, indispensable capability offered by the Company. Click "Send."

Distribution Plans

- Regularly scheduled, well-advertised free seminars and demonstrations will be held throughout each service territory. Attendees will be registered in advance and at the door, for future prospect marketing. Seminars will be held in hotel conference rooms. Subscribers will be signed at the conclusion of the seminars, and future appointments will be set with other seminar attendees.
- Subscriber network sold directly, face-to-face, by experienced and skilled commissioned sales representatives. Sales force will be trained regarding construction industry requirements and network technology.
- A direct subscription form available on the Company's Web site.

Several experienced construction sales representatives have committed to the company once seed funding has been secured. As more service territories are added, more sales personnel will be added. The sales force will be aggressive and trained in construction needs and online network technology.

Beta testing of the network will be performed in the chosen test-bed market.

Pricing Strategies

Monthly tiered subscriber fees will range from $100 to $ 595 per month, depending on the extent of service required by the subscribing company. At an average of $300 per month, these fees are approximately 20 percent higher than common plan room monthly fees. Tiers of service will include:

Plan One—$100. For small contractors and suppliers who require limited information, it will provide only public bid announcements.

Plan Two—$250, Limited geographic area plan. Offers all projects placed for bid. It includes online updates and new bid proposals.

Plan Three—$200 per area. Access to projects and jobs in additional service territories.

Plan Four—$595, Unlimited network access. All services above plus company Virtual Private Network (Intranet). Private information and communications services, within the company only, by authorized employees.

Options—On-screen estimating. Takeoff capabilities, material and dimension, for all projects in the service territory. This is in addition to the other services. One-time software cost plus monthly fees ranging from $25 to $100.

New customer price incentives will be offered according to market survey findings.

Marketing Strategy

Target Markets

1. Construction contractors (subcontractors and suppliers)
2. Engineering firms
3. Architects

Initial Action Plan

The first two months sales' activity will be handled by the Company's president to enable him to fully assess the sales process. In month three, a contract "commission only" salesperson will be retained. First year's projections call for adding 30 new accounts per month. New sales commissions will be 20 percent of the initial month plus a 5 percent override for each month thereafter. The Company will provide salespersons with a flat $1,000 per month expense allowance to cover auto and entertainment expenses.

The Company believes that the sales process is more awareness and education than selling. The Company will support sales efforts by offering a number of customer benefits (see Strategy). Sales will be made on a company rather than an individual basis. This means that a company can sign up for a Plan Four package and any number of individuals can access the program.

Strategy

Active personal attention to customers. Finding their wants and needs, and meeting them.

Promoted and advertised on a continuous basis. Free seminars and demonstrations to show how the Company's system will benefit the customer. Q&A sessions at end will allow for free flow of information. The intent is to "humanize" the company, and place the customer more at ease.

Subscribers will be signed at end of meetings. A customer database will be created for all potential customers.

- Highest quality company management and accounting services will be in place.
- Complete cooperation with—and marketing to—architects and engineers, whose original CAD plans will be needed for the network.
- Open house social events on a regular basis to promote networking for existing customers (and their colleagues).
- Garner support from AGC industry professionals through local trade newsletters, association meetings, and conferences. Make presentations at key meetings.
- Regularly distribute substantive newsletter to include local media outlets. Establish sound working relationships with key industry and media personnel.
- Advertize through direct mail, Internet, and "e-zines."
- Develop targeted Internet marketing programs and strategies.
- Network open 24/7 for greater value to the customer.
- Friendly, personal training of network subscribers.
- Easy-to-use online Help system.

Management

Officers and Directors

Jack Edwards, founder and president. Jack has an extensive background in both the construction industry and computers. All through high school and college, he worked in his father's general construction firm as it progressed from residential and small commercial jobs to large multifaceted projects. Jack's experience included job takeoffs and estimating. His college education was focused on math and computers. While working as a project manager with his father's firm after college, he recognized the need for a better way to review plans and prepare job estimates, and the problems that arise from errors in this process. Consequently, he began to develop the software and research the components needed to implement the Company's current construction-oriented systems.

Jack has taken advantage of his industry and college connections and has assembled a number of key advisers who assist him in troubleshooting and adding improvements to the current system.

1. **Jerry Mitchell** is a construction attorney with the firm of Boyd, Mellon and Laprizzi of Houston, Texas. He is a graduate of the University of Texas School of Law. Jerry advises the Company on construction legal issues.

2. **Ms. Irene Takahashi** is an information technology specialist and graduate of the University of Southern California. She is a former IS manager and programmer for the Loral Corporation and Lockheed-Martin Corporation. Irene has overseen the development of The Delivery™ System. She will work full-time on system updates, management, and maintenance.

3. **Mr. Fred Wagshul** is a database programmer and internet technology expert. Fred is a graduate of the University of Minnesota who worked for the Casa Grande Materials Co. in Albuquerque, New Mexico, before establishing Kingston Designs, an independent, databases-driven Intranet company. The Delivery™ System is built from a Kingston Designs template. Fred will advise on and write code for various changes and updates necessary for system operations.

4. **Ms. Janet Washington** is the assistant marketing director at Washington University in St. Louis, Missouri. She advises Construction Delivery Corporation on marketing and financial strategies on a contract basis.

5. **Mr. Ralph Bellman** is a construction industry expert, with more than 20 years of experience running contract bids and site supervision for the Empire State Construction Company, a large, regional construction firm in New York City. On a part-time, long term, contract basis, he will assist the Company in finding firms who will register blueprints on the Delivery Web site.

6. **Mr. Tom Watkins** is the executive director of the International Association of Plumbing Contractors. He will act as an adviser to the Company on marketing, sales, and registration.

7. **Tsu Wah Kee** is a highly experienced construction industry builder and designer, and a graduate of Kim Poo University in South Korea. He consults to the electrical power industry worldwide, including Pacific Gas & Electric, Commonwealth Edison, Tennessee Valley Authority, Western Power Administration, and Japan Nuclear Power Agency. He will assist the Company by registering plans to the site and helping to establish its presence in the electrical power industry.

Professional Advisers

> **Mr. John Howard,** Howard and Associates, CPA
> **Mr. Sam Jardine, Esq.,** attorney
> **Ms. Demeter Jenkins,** investment banker

Financial

Overview

> The Company has authorized one million shares of common stock of which it has issued 200 thousand shares to its president as sole shareholder. A pro forma balance sheet would indicate that the company has total assets of approximately $150,000 including computer hardware and the capitalization of some of its proprietary software programs.
>
> Pro forma projections shown a maximum $60,000 cash flow deficiency. The Company has secured a line of credit from a local bank of $75,000 secured by its assets and personally guaranteed by the president to cover its first year operations.
>
> The president intends to access the potential of expanding the Company's operations at month nine and is hopeful of adding new areas and exploring the potential of growing the Company to a nationwide concern.

Pro Forma Projections

> Pro forma projections are attached in an abbreviated format and include the first year month-by-month and the second year by quarters. These projections include revenues, sales/marketing, general/administrative, and a combination profit/taxes and simple cumulative cash flow.

Year One

Month	1	2	3	4	5	6	7	8
Revenues								
Number of units online	10	30	60	90	110	140	170	200
At $300 average	$ 3,000	$ 9,000	$ 18,000	$ 27,000	$ 33,000	$ 42,000	$ 51,000	$ 60,000
Sales/Marketing								
Commissions, new sales			1,800	1,800	1,800	1,800	1,800	1,800
Commissions, overrides = 5%				1,350	1,650	2,100	2,550	3,000
Sales expense reimbursement		2,000		1,000	1,000	1,000	1,000	1,000
Literature		2,000				500		
Advertising/promotion		5,000		3,000		3,000		3,000
Subtotal		4,000	1,800	4,150	4,450	5,400	5,350	5,800
General and Administrative								
Owner	5,000	5,000	5,000	5,000	5,000	5,000	5,000	5,000
Webmaster	4,000	4,000	4,000	4,000	4,000	4,000	4,000	4,000
Asst. Webmaster(s)						3,000	3,000	3,000
Admin. Asst.				2,000	2,000	2,000	2,000	2,000
Payrole burden (25%)	2,250	2,250	2,250	2,750	2,750	3,500	3,500	3,500
Office lease	1,500	1,500	1,500	1,500	1,500	1,500	1,500	1,500
Office furniture lease	4,000			2,000			2,000	
Computer lease/maintance	8,000	2,200	2,200	2,200	2,200	2,200	2,200	2,200
Office equip. lease/maint.	800	800	800	800	800	800	800	800
Phone, voice and data	1,500	1,500	1,500	1,500	1,500	1,500	1,500	1,500
Accounting/legal	1,500	500	500	500	500	500	500	500
Consulting	1,000	1,000	1,000	3,000	1,000	1,000	3,000	1,000
Travel and Entertainment	500	1,000	1,000	1,000	1,000	1,000	1,000	1,000
Insurance	300	300	300	300	300	300	300	300
Contract software updates			1,000	1,000	1,000	1,000	1,000	1,000
Office supplies	1,000	400	400	400	400	400	400	400
Postage	200	200	400	200	200	500	200	200
Newsletter, edit/print			2,000			2,000		
Licenses/dues/memberships/ subscriptions	300	300	300	300	300	600	300	300
Miscellaneous	500	500	500	500	500	500	500	500
Bank charges/bad debts (1.5% sales)	45	135	270	405	495	630	765	900
Subtotal	$ 32,395	$ 21,585	$ 24,920	$ 29,355	$ 25,445	$ 31,930	$ 33,465	$ 29,600
Total expenses	$ 32,395	$ 25,585	$ 26,720	$ 33,505	$ 29,895	$ 37,330	$ 38,815	$ 35,400
Pretax profit	$(29,395)	$(16,585)	$ (8,720)	$ (6,505)	$ 3,105	$ 4,670	$ 12,185	$ 24,600
Taxes @ 35%					$ 1,087	$ 1,635	$ 4,265	$ 8,610
(Tax carry-forward)	(29,395)	(45,980)	(54,700)	(61,205)	(58,100)	(53,430)	(41,245)	(16,645)
Net profit after taxes	$(29,395)	$(16,585)	$ (8,720)	$ (6,505)	$ 2,018	$ 3,036	$ 7,920	$ 15,990
Profit % after tax	−980%	−184%	−48%	−24%	6%	7%	16%	27%
Cummulative cash flow	$(29,395)	$(45,980)	$(54,700)	$(61,205)	$(59,187)	$(56,151)	$(48,231)	$(32,241)

Assumptions

Unit sales: Programs are priced from $100 to $595 per month. An average sales of $300 is assumed.

Revenues: Unit sales increase by 30 new accounts per month after second month at $300 average per sale. Year 2 add 15 new per month.

Commissions: salesperson (starting month three) gets 20% each new sales and 5% monthly override. Year 2 = straight 20%.

Sales expense reimbursment: $1,000 per month for auto, entertainment. Year 2 = 7% of sales.

Advertising/promotion: Will sponsor networking parties every two months.

Postage: 200/month plus newsletter every three months.

Appendix

					Year Two				
9	**10**	**11**	**12**	**Totals**	**Q1**	**Q2**	**Q3**	**Q4**	**Totals**
230	260	290	310	1,900	355	400	445	490	5,070
$69,000	$78,000	$87,000	$ 93,000	$570,000	$319,500	$360,000	$400,500	$441,000	$1,521,000
1,800	1,800	1,800	1,800	$ 18,000	47,925	54,000	60,075	66,150	$ 304,200
3,450	3,900	4,350	4,650	$ 27,000					
1,000	1,000	1,000	1,000	$ 11,000	3,355	3,780	4,205	4,631	$ 21,294
			500	$ 3,000	2,000	2,000	2,000	2,000	$ 8,000
	3,000		3,000	$ 20,000	5,000	5,000	5,000	5,000	$ 20,000
6,250	6,700	7,150	7,950	$ 59,000	53,280	59,780	66,280	72,781	$ 252,121
5,000	5,000	5,000	5,000	$ 60,000	24,000	24,000	24,000	24,000	$ 96,000
4,000	4,000	4,000	4,000	$ 48,000	20,000	20,000	20,000	20,000	$ 80,000
3,000	3,000	3,000	3,000	$ 21,000	18,000	24,000	3,000	36,000	$ 108,000
2,000	2,000	3,000	3,000	$ 20,000	12,000	15,000	18,000	21,000	$ 66,000
3,500	3,500	3,750	3,750	$ 37,250	9,000	9,750	10,500	11,250	$ 40,500
1,500	1,500	1,500	1,500	$ 18,000	6,000	6,000	6,000	6,000	$ 24,000
	2,000			$ 10,000	3,000	3,000	3,000	3,000	$ 12,000
2,200	2,200	2,200	2,200	$ 32,200	10,500	10,500	13,000	13,000	$ 47,000
800	800	800	800	$ 9,600	3,000	3,000	3,000	3,000	$ 12,000
1,500	1,500	1,500	1,500	$ 18,000	6,000	9,000	12,000	15,000	$ 42,000
500	500	500	1,500	$ 8,000	2,500	2,500	2,500	5,000	$ 12,500
1,000	3,000	1,000	1,000	$ 18,000	5,000	5,000	5,000	5,000	$ 20,000
1,000	1,000	1,000	1,000	$ 11,500	4,000	6,000	6,000	8,000	$ 24,000
300	300	300	300	$ 3,600	1,200	1,200	1,200	1,200	$ 4,800
1,000	1,000	1,000	1,000	$ 10,000	6,000	6,000	8,000	8,000	$ 28,000
400	400	400	400	$ 5,400	2,000	2,500	3,000	3,500	$ 11,000
600	200	200	800	$ 3,900	1,500	1,800	2,100	2,400	$ 7,800
2,000			2,000	$ 8,000	3,000	4,000	5,000	6,000	$ 18,000
300	300	300	300	$ 3,900	1,200	1,200	1,500	1,500	$ 5,400
500	500	500	500	$ 6,000	2,000	2,000	2,000	2,000	$ 8,000
1,035	1,170	1,305	1,395	$ 8,550	4,792	5,400	6,008	6,615	$ 22,815
$ 32,135	$33,870	$31,255	$ 34,945	$360,900	144,692	161,850	181,808	201,465	$ 689,815
$ 38,385	$40,570	$38,405	$ 42,895	$419,900	$197,972	$221,630	$248,088	$274,246	$ 941,936
$ 30,615	$37,430	$48,595	$ 50,105	$150,100	$121,528	$138,370	$152,412	$166,755	$ 579,065
$ 10,715	$13,101	$17,008	$ 17,537	$ 73,957	$ 42,535	$ 48,430	$ 53,344	$ 58,364	$ 202,673
13,970	51,400	99,995	150,100	300,200					
$ 19,900	$24,330	$31,587	$ 32,568	$ 76,143	$ 78,993	$ 89,941	$ 99,068	$108,390	$ 376,392
29%	31%	36%	35%	13%	25%	25%	25%	25%	25%
$(12,341)	$11,988	$43,575	$ 76,143						

Index